9-3-17.

To Debra.

I pray te
have state
stength.

Blessus
Rut P.

SAY YES TO NEW OPPORTUNITIES!

BE MOTIVATED TO L.E.A.R.N.

RUTH PEARSON

authorHOUSE®

AuthorHouse™ UK
1663 Liberty Drive
Bloomington, IN 47403 USA
www.authorhouse.co.uk
Phone: 0800.197.4150

Published by AuthorHouse 02/10/2017

ISBN: 978-1-5246-7661-2 (sc)
ISBN: 978-1-5246-7662-9 (hc)
ISBN: 978-1-5246-7660-5 (e)

Print information available on the last page.

Any people depicted in stock imagery provided by Thinkstock are models,
and such images are being used for illustrative purposes only.
Certain stock imagery © Thinkstock.

This book is printed on acid-free paper.

Dedication

I would like to dedicate this book to my loving mothers, Onelle Weekes and Gloria Hudson, my sister, Oneta Letang, and brother, Charles Mtonga. You have been my inspiration.

I wouldn't have accomplished so many things in my life without your support and direction.

Contents

Foreword

Sometimes, life can seem like a roller coaster; during the downs, we can often feel frustrated and confused. One of the best questions to ask ourselves at that point is, what is critical for me to resolve right now? Not tomorrow, but right now. What is the one thing I need help with, so that I am able to get out of this down, take the next step, and move on up?

It can sometimes be easier to think about what you want the future to look like than to deal with the challenges you are facing right now. This is where time with a Master Coach can change everything. Great coaches will help you go from where you are currently to where you want to be, and they can do that in a very short period of time. In some instances, one session is all you need. Coaching is an active process and not a passive one.

Tony and I first met Ruth Pearson when she attended one of our Master Coach training weekends. Life had certainly thrown her, as she calls it, several curve balls, and she was very confused as to what she should do next with her career. She had been a teacher for over twenty-five years but wanted to explore new opportunities outside of the classroom. The Ruth we see today at our training events is totally transformed from the Ruth we met at the first training course. She is very confident and focused, having been on a remarkable journey of discovery in a relatively short period of time.

If your life is a roller coaster right now and you would like to learn to focus on quickly overcoming the challenges, so you can achieve your goals and take advantage of new opportunities, I encourage you to read this book. You will discover hidden gems about yourself, as you too learn to say yes to new opportunities.

I wish you a great future.
Nicki Vee
Tony & Nicki Vee's Master Coach

to learn and teachers who would not embrace new educational strategies. When I returned to the United Kingdom, I completed my studies. Don't be fearful; this book is not about the challenges that are occurring in the British education system, so please read on.

When I returned from my holiday, I gained a few teaching roles, but I was not able to make a difference, as I did before. Despite me putting into practice all of my years experiences working in education, in February 2015, I had an emotional meltdown while at my school. This resulted in me taking two months off from work. I felt that my life had fallen apart, and I wouldn't be able to rebuild it. That was not the case, as you will see. The bad experiences I went through became the catalyst for remarkable changes in my life. I started to share with others how low I had become but also how I used the learning I gained in a positive way. I became an inspiration to them. I taught them that they too could overcome challenges in their lives by being willing to step outside their comfort zones.

As part of my recovery, at home from work, I attended a personal development seminar in April 2015. This was something new for me, but from the information sent about the training, I thought I would be able to gain some answers to how I was feeling. This was the first time I was absent from work for months, other than a lupus flare-up or physical illness. I was home for work-related stress.

So, what happened that day? The day I fell off the tightrope and ended up in a deep pit.

I was in school teaching my classes, as usual. Some of the comments that the students shared with me in the morning worried me, *"If you think the way we treat you is bad, you should see how we have treated other teachers who have taught us."* They thought making comments like this, was acceptable. I should feel good that I was treated better than other teachers! In the next class I had, some students were upset, because I refused to have a disruptive student return to my class, before a meeting with their parent.

The students' behaviour deteriorated; each class grew worse than the one before. I tried taking deep breaths to calm myself down. Lunchtime came, and I thought that the afternoon classes would be better. I was teaching year 11 students, and they had an important examination the following week. It was worth 25% of their final grade and if they failed the examination, they would fail the course. I spent my lunchtime preparing the room for the mock examination. The papers were laid out on the desks including the equipment they would need -pens, pencils, rulers.

The first students came into the classroom and took their places. The students who had been previously removed from the class for their disruptive behaviour, came in and started shouting. *"Why do we need to do this test?" "We do not want to do this course."*

I thought to myself, *"Why should student's grades suffer because a minority of voices are more powerful than their one?"*

I left the classroom in the care of the teaching assistants and went into the prep room to make a call, to have the disruptive students removed from the classroom, according to the school's behaviour policy.

Instead of making the call, I broke down and began crying uncontrollably. I felt completely disempowered. I knew that the students were in control of my classroom and there was nothing that I could do or say to change the situation. They knew that too, which was why they had been so bold with their comments. I also felt unsafe. I had already had a couple of the students, in my face swearing at me, on a previous occasion, and nothing had happened to them. I was like a pressure cooker that was about to burst, but I did not know.

What happened was completely unexpected and was not the way that I normally dealt with stressful situations. Crying in public was not like me. I felt light-headed, and the room was spinning. I felt like I was going to collapse onto the concrete floor. One of my colleagues had come out of her classroom at the same time, and she held me in her arms and helped me to sit down safely. I was crying uncontrollably, like a young child. She could not believe the emotional state that she found me in, as she had always seen me as a strong person. This experience was the straw that broke the camel's back, as the saying goes. She had to return to her class, so she rang the office and explained what had happened and asked for assistance for me. They sent help, and after I had calmed myself down, I left school early. I used my own internal resilience to get myself home. I didn't want to remain in the school or, worst still, be taken to hospital.

If you knew me personally, you would know that this reaction is not typical for me; actually, it's very rare that anyone will see me cry in public and especially not for an issue to do with students.

The next day, I visited my doctor. I was still feeling overwhelmed with all of my emotions. In his surgery, I broke down in tears, once again. I shared with him that I was afraid of doing the one occupation that I had done for the last twenty-five years. I was scared to go back into a classroom with students. Dr Smith, not his real name, became very concerned, because he had never seen me in his office in tears, despite helping me through many painful situations since 2001. As he recorded detailed notes, he gave me a medical certificate for a month off and had his receptionist give me the number of the local counselling services. He also advised that I should return to see him at the end of the month. I left the surgery, perplexed and in deep emotional pain, and returned home. My mind was spinning, as I tried to understand what was happening to me.

I am usually a very confident and independent person who doesn't let life's challenges knock me down. This behaviour was totally out of my character. I had no reference point. I also grappled with what I was going to tell my family and friends to explain why I was home from work. They knew it was not a holiday, and they knew I was conscientious and dedicated towards work, especially when I have examination classes. As it was a Friday, I decided that I would face these issues on Monday morning. Over the weekend, I developed a chesty cough and a pain in my left side, so I now had an excuse as to why I would be home, at least for the first week.

When I arrived home from the doctor on Friday morning, I called the counselling services. When I first called, there was no one at the other end, and I was required to leave a message. I put the phone down without leaving one. In my mind, I convinced myself that I had completed the call. However, I had a deep nagging feeling, so I picked up the phone again and rang and left a message. Within an hour, my call was returned, and I spoke with a reassuring counsellor. At the end of the call, I laid down and went to sleep. This was the first proper sleep that I had since the incident had occurred.

I was now faced with another challenge. I was home from work, and I now had all of these new emotions to deal with. What was I going to do with my time, to keep myself busy? Busyness was one of my distraction strategies, so that I don't have to deal with real issues. Compounding this, I felt immense feelings of anger inside. In my head, I was thinking if the situation had been handled in a different way, I would still be at work, doing a job that I liked and not at home, feeling hurt, inadequate, and angry. Being angry was a new emotion I was dealing with; that was also compounding the situation.

That was when this book was conceived. As I recovered at home, I used the same skills that I had learnt in my studies and applied them to my personal situation. I knew I needed an occupation to use my skills, if I was not going to return to teaching. From this low point, I realised that I could help others with similar experiences to my own. Exactly how I would do this, I did not know at the time, but something deep within me was driving me forward. This is what the core message of this book is about. It's my journey back to wholeness and a new passion in life. As you read, I hope that you will be encouraged and feel that you too can reach for the next level (whatever that means personally for you).

I reflect back on how I was feeling. I was depressed and an emotional wreck. For days, I carried these emotions, and then I had a breakthrough. I took a personal development book from my shelf and started to read it. The book showed me how I could use my skills in a new way. As I read the book, I started to heal. Not big steps but in little ways. I found that I was no longer crying and disconnecting myself from everyone around me. The book reinforced that we all have challenges in our lives; some are expected but most are not, and what makes the difference is how we deal with these challenges. I realised that I had a choice to make. I could dwell on the situation I was facing, or I could use the experiences as part of my self-development. I also learnt I could help others to face challenging times in their lives in a positive way.

Following this breakthrough, I awoke the next day with a new attitude. I decided that I was going to use these challenges as steppingstones. I would stand on the stones instead of letting the stones crush my spirit. I knew that the weeks and months ahead wouldn't be easy, as I would have some major decisions to make regarding my future. Teaching, a job that I had always been passionate about, was no longer possible because of what I was now facing. A close friend was concerned, as she too had noticed that my enthusiasm for teaching was waning. This was not the first time that I had worked in a challenging school, so that was not the reason for my feelings.

I will share with you a previous experience that I had working in a challenging school. In September 2008, I left a good job to take up a leadership post in a school in North London. If you looked at their statistics, you wouldn't have willingly taught at the school, but I wanted to make a difference in the lives of these young people, and I had the skills the school was looking for at the time. After I had been there for a few days, I was called into a classroom and was faced with a student who was bigger, taller, and stronger than me. I was expected to remove her from the classroom and take her to another room. When I arrived at the classroom, she asked, "What are you going to do about my behaviour?" I had two choices: stand my ground or run away (if not physically, mentally). I stood my ground and escorted her out of the room.

I remember sharing the incident with another member of the senior leadership team. She assured me that things would get better. The students would test me. She reminded me that I had joined the school to make a difference in the lives of the young people, and their families, by giving them a chance in life. My presence there would motivate them to learn, if not initially, by the end of the school year. With this positive attitude, I continued my role. Within a short time, I realised I was transforming the behaviour and attitude of the students and also some of the staff. Within six months, I was promoted from assistant head teacher to deputy head teacher.

I had a thirst for learning new things and then putting this knowledge into practice. Once I had become an expert, then I would share the knowledge with others, as I wanted them to develop as well. Unlike the Dead Sea, which has water flowing into it but no outlet, as I learnt information, I would share it with others; this allowed us all to develop. I have used this same strategy in this book. I have recorded in detail the learning that I went through in my transitions, so you can apply this learning to your own personal and professional decisions.

I found healing and a new perspective in life by reading a personal development book. I hope that as you read this book and learn about my experiences and hear my reflective thoughts, you too will gain an in-depth understanding of where you currently are and the steps that you can take on your personal journey as an active learner.

As I read that personal development book, I knew my experiences were not unique to an educational setting. They occur in several types of businesses. It was from this feeling of pain that the idea for this book was born: *Say Yes to New Opportunities*.

Although there are many complex issues involved in these questions, both within an education setting and within organisations, one common thread we discovered was the level of motivation within the individuals, especially when they were facing challenges that were either personal or professional – or both.

I discovered that being motivated is for everyone, not just for individuals in an education setting. As newborns, we use motivation to learn about our environment. As children, we learn by being persistent. Imagine when you were learning to walk and fell the first time. You had a choice to make. You could get up and try again, or you could just stay seated on the ground. To be able to walk, you made the decision to try again until you were successful.

We are going to take a journey together. As we start off, ask yourself this question: *"Do I have the same tenacity that I had when I was a child learning something new?"*

The strategies learnt in this book will be relevant to you no matter what sector you are employed in. You may be having challenges in your personal life. From my interactions with individuals and my own personal experiences, I have learnt about the importance of motivation, and for the remainder of this book, I would like to share these experiences with you.

What Is Motivation, and Why Is It Important?

Have you ever stopped to think why you act or behave in a particular way? The reason you behave in each situation is what motivation is about. Motivation is what drives you to do a task. What gives you a buzz for doing the various activities that you carry out daily? What are you working on at 3 a.m., knowing that you will not get any financial reward for it? Motivation is what causes you to act, whether it's getting a glass of water to reduce thirst or reading a book to gain knowledge.

It's essential to know why you behave a particular way in a situation. Your actions are complex; they are due to a number of internal and external factors that have affected you in the past as well as what you are currently experiencing. What are these factors, and how do they influence you as an individual? These questions were asked by Abraham Maslow, an American psychologist.

Maslow is best known for creating a pyramid model that explains what motivates people, from their basic to their higher needs. This model is called "Maslow's Hierarchy of Needs." The model is divided into two areas: basic needs and growth needs. He found that if your basic needs are not met, then you will not be able to grow physically, socially, mentally, and so on. Also, you will not be able to embrace new opportunities as they come in your direction.

The original model had five stages, but due to further studies, the new model now has eight stages. It has been found that only 1 percent of people reach the highest level, which Maslow called self-actualisation.

Your basic needs are biological and physiological. These needs are clean air, food, water, a suitable home, and warmth. You will not be able to survive and thrive without these needs being met. These are your foundational needs.

Your next level of need is to be safe from internal and external dangers. Each country has local and national laws to protect its citizens. You also carry out specific actions to make sure your homes and possessions are safe. Within your own personal life, you need stable relationships, where you are free from fear and danger.

The third level is for love and belonging. You need to have people in your life who are dependable. You need love and affection from friends and family. When you have romantic relationships, you also have a need for intimacy.

The fourth level deals with your esteem. You first need to have respect for yourself – self-respect – as well as respect from others. We all have areas that we have achieved well in, and as you spend more time developing your own skills, you have the potential to become an expert. This raises your status as you interrelate with others.

The final level in Maslow's hierarchy is self-actualisation. At this level, all the earlier needs have been fully met, and you have found your true purpose in life. You have an internal peace and happiness. Even though challenges may come in your life, you have the skills and support, both within and without, to achieve personal growth.

Other needs that were added between the fourth and fifth levels are shown below. The first of these needs is called "cognitive needs." As humans, we have a natural need to learn new things; to explore the world around us; to discover new things and use this knowledge in the creation of our own things. This is why everyday objects, for example mobile phones, are being developed with more and more functions, to enhance their use in our personal and professional lives.

The next level is aesthetic needs. One of the reasons we go on holiday is to discover new places of beauty. Whilst you are away, you have a better work-life balance and can appreciate the new surroundings and internal peace that often comes with it. This environment can also lead to a greater feeling of intimacy within your relationships.

Maslow divided the top layer to add a new need, which he called self-transcendence. This is also referred to as spiritual needs. These needs are based around beliefs and values. These include values such as being authentic and having integrity. Integrity is a core value for a happy and successful life. If you have integrity, you will be totally honest and truthful in every area of our life. As well as developing yourself, you will have the natural desire to help others achieve their own personal goals. You will also contribute to the lives of others, even those who are not in a position to repay you. My core values are integrity, being authentic, and nurturing others.

Now that you have a better understanding of how our environment and relationships affect your level of motivation, and how you can move from one level to the next, depending on internal and external factors, let's apply this knowledge to yourself. Start the journey of discovering your own level of motivation.

This will be our first interactive exercise. You will be asked four questions, and for each one, you need to select response (a), (b), or (c). The responses will give you an initial baseline for your level of motivation. Answer each question honestly. Do not spend too much time thinking about your response. The first answer that you connect with usually is your honest response.

Question One

You attend a training course about an area of work that you identified during your appraisal meeting. Do you

(a) not attend because the notice given to you was too short?
(b) attend and engage with the tasks set during the training?
(c) attend and apply the knowledge to the area that you identified in your appraisal when you return to work?

Question Two

You attend a training seminar and receive a manual with useful information. What do you do with the manual once you return to work?

(a) Put it on a shelf or in your filing cabinet.
(b) Go over the notes that you made to reinforce the learning you received.
(c) Go over your notes and then share the main points learnt with other colleagues.

Question Three

You are looking for a new job and find a role that you have always wanted to do. As you read the job description, you are unsure if you have all of the skills and standards required. Do you

(a) decide not to apply for the job because you tell yourself that you will not be shortlisted?
(b) apply and wait to see if you are shortlisted for the interview?
(c) contact the company to gain clarification, and then use the information given to complete the application and apply for the role?

Question Four

You are asked to attend the interview. On your arrival, you see that you are one of six candidates for the post. As you share information with each other, you feel the other five candidates are more experienced than you. What do you do next?

(a) After you complete the first selection task, which you found difficult, you withdraw from the selection process.

(b) You complete all of the selection tasks to the best of your ability.

(c) You complete the selection tasks to the best of your ability, and during the interview stage, you answer all of the questions confidently, using information that you researched about the company.

In each of the four situations above, the candidates have exactly the same opportunities, but their outcome will be different depending on the choices they made and their own personal level of motivation.

Motivational Maps

As I shared with you in the introduction, one of the turning points in my mindset was the results that I obtained when I completed my own Motivational Map. My report allowed me to discover that I am more motivated and happy at work when my core motivators are met. My core motivators are based on my personality, my beliefs, and the expectations of others.

I completed the map in March 2015, when I was going through a challenging time in my life. I was looking for clarity. The map identified motivators of work which are found within cluster groups. More information about the use of these maps is found on their main website. The details are found in the Useful Links chapter.

As I completed my profile, I found that my primary motivator was searching for meaning in the activities I engaged in. I seek to make a difference in the lives of others. If this motivator is not met, then it could affect me adversely. I now knew why I reacted the way I did earlier in the year, when the students in my classes didn't want to learn and had made me feel unsafe and vulnerable, and also when I was made redundant. I also understood why I worked so hard in my role as deputy head teacher. Even though I was having to work late nights and the work was highly stressful, due to the fact that the school was in special measures, I was still motivated to go to work each day. Working in a school in special measures meant a lot more challenges and pressure for teachers and students. Our work was always being monitored by Ofsted, the local authority, and the dioceses, as we were a faith-based school. Despite all of this additional work, I gladly completed my areas of work, because I knew that I was personally changing lives and giving students opportunities that they would not have had. I was motivated to continue by the changes I saw in their opportunities (I saw some of them apply for good colleges to continue their studies, either studying A levels or BTEC Level Three qualifications). Our school was being rewarded with increased attainment and student progress, especially the ones who made the conscious decision they wanted to do well at school and leave with good qualifications. At the time all of these challenges were taking place, I completed my National Professional Qualification for Headship (NPQH). The year after the school closed, I graduated with a distinction grade in MA Education. As you can see, I enjoy learning and applying what I learn to my professional and personal decisions.

I realised from all of these experiences that I worked in education because I liked learning new things and using that knowledge to make a positive difference in the lives of others. Now in my new roles as a well-being coach, motivational speaker, author, and television presenter, I am applying the new skills that I am learning in new settings. What is core to all of my work and roles, I am making a positive difference in the lives of others.

Let me share an experience of how a coaching session changed the life of one of my clients. I will call the client Sarah. I first met Sarah when I ran my seminar called "Five Steps to Overcoming Challenges." At the end of the seminar, she underwent a series of coaching sessions with me. Sarah was feeling very demotivated at work, due to the constant pressure. Her department had downsized after government cuts, but the workload was still excessive. They were having to work long hours at the office and also bring work home. There was no work-life balance, and consequently, her health was beginning to suffer. At our initial coaching session, we spoke about this as a critical area in her life that she needed to address right away: her work-life balance. We explored what was currently happening, examined the effects it was having in multiple areas of her life, and assessed what the consequences would be if no changes were made. She was able to explore the decisions she needed to make for herself. In subsequent sessions, we explored in detail the new opportunities that were taking place in her life as a result of her taking action.

For the final session, we completed her motivational map. When she received her report, she was pleased to see that she had a high level of motivation, but also, she was able to understand the reasons why she had been so demotivated with work in the past. She was taking responsibility for her work-life balance and had become an active learner.

Active and Passive Learners

Let's return to the four questions that you were previously given. Be honest with yourself. Did you complete them? If not, why not? If you did, did you answer them quickly or did you put thought into your answers?

In both my work in education and now working in other organisations as a trainer and coach, I have discovered that there are two types of learners: active learners and passive learners. If you are an active learner, you will engage 100 percent with the learning activity. You will actively take part in the decision-making process. You will also apply the knowledge you learn to multiple situations. You will utilise high-level thinking processes: analysis, problem solving, and experimenting. You try new ideas, and you are creative. You will be highly motivated and intentional about your learning. This contrasts with a passive learner, who may or may not take in new information shared with them. They will not typically engage with others. They do not impact with others positively, share insights, or contribute to their own learning or that of others.

What type of learner are you? You have a choice as to the type of learner you are. If you are a passive learner, you can make changes to become a more active learner. To get the most out of this book, you will need to be an active learner. You will need to honestly answer questions and carry out tasks like the questionnaire above. Now that you have made the choice to be an active learner, we can move onto the next chapter, which introduces you to S.T.E.P.S.

Summary

In this chapter, we have learnt the following:

- The impact of being motivated, or not motivated, in our personal and professional lives, and how motivation has affected us from our childhood,
- What is motivation and why it's important to us,
- A raised awareness of motivation and how we can apply it to our own lives,
- Ways that motivation can be assessed, including the use of Motivation Maps, and
- Ways to evaluate if you are an active or passive learner.

Action Points

- Complete the questionnaire, if you have not done so already.
- Evaluate what type of learner you are and write down at least two steps that you can take to make yourself a more active learner.

Chapter 2

S.T.E.P.S.: FIVE STEPS TO MOTIVATE YOU TO TAKE ACTION

Overview of S.T.E.P.S.

In the last chapter, we learnt about the topic of motivation. We also learnt what passive and active learners look like and how you can become a more active learner. As you continued reading, I hope that you discovered, if you did not know it beforehand, that you are now an active learner.

In this chapter, we are going to learn five steps you can adopt to motivate you to take action. In my life, I have faced a lot of challenges around the topics of health, work, family, and finances, just to name a few. At times, these have left me feeling really low and, if I am really honest with myself, in a state of depression. This low feeling has lasted anything from a few days to several months. I may be so low I don't even register that I am feeling depressed. When I am feeling depressed and so low, usually one thing will happen: A conversation, something I read, or something I hear on the television causes me stop and think. I may act on this prompting immediately, but in most cases, the prompting has to be numerous. Each time, it needs to become more insistent for me to take notice.

At that time, I start to reflect on what is happening, and something jolts me to take action. The action usually is something small, but because of the impact it has on me, it becomes a big action. After I take this step and see the benefit, I have a choice to make: Am I going to remain where I am, or am I going to take action and do something differently? We cannot expect our situation to change if we always do things the same way.

You too may be feeling low, feeling depressed, or just feeling out of sorts. The reading of this book may be the stimulus you need to take the next steps in your life, whatever those steps need to be. Remember, it was the reading of a personal development book that jolted me out of a state of depression. The main decision I want you to make right now is to do something positive. The actual activity you carry out is not what is important. What is important is you do something positive. We often forget that if we do not make a conscious choice to change something, then our indecision is still an action.

As I continued to reflect on and review my own personal situation, I realised that I had put into place a similar set of strategies to lift myself out of my low feelings and negative state of mind. I am going to share this route with you now. I call it my five-step strategy to motivate you. I apply this strategy to different areas of my life, but here I am going to use the steps in the context of motivation. The order of the steps might be different, but what is consistent is the actions I need to take to apply the five steps to a given scenario.

In the introduction, I shared with you an incident that resulted in me having an emotional breakdown. For the first time in my life, I felt totally demotivated from a job that I had loved for over twenty-five years. I realised that I could not remain in a similar role, as I was slowly dying inside. I had to do something. I had to take the first step. So the first step of the five is **Start**.

On a scale from 0 to 10, where 0 is feeling totally demotivated and 10 is feeling highly motivated, how would you score? I was at a 0.

If you too have scored yourself low, what decisions should you take? I realised that I had to be honest with myself and say I was not happy with my situation. I felt like I was attending my first meeting at Alcoholics Anonymous, and it was my turn to stand up, say my name, and admit in public that I was an alcoholic. My secret was now out in the open.

Even though the people who attend AA are scared of making this initial declaration, they feel a great sense of relief when they eventually stand up and say, "*My name is [insert name], and I am an alcoholic.*" They have finally admitted to themselves that they have a problem, but they have also admitted to a group of people that they want to change. Their mindset can now start to change from dwelling on negative thoughts to having some positive thoughts. They have made a decision to change where they currently are and put into action steps to start a new journey in their life. As they make this decision, they may be one of the few who never return to drinking alcohol again, but for many, they will have to go through the process several times.

Ask yourself the question, *"What do you want, or need, to do differently in your life?"*

Don't just skim over the question. Take some time and reflect on what you want to change. Remember: It doesn't have to be anything large. You could decide that you want to go to bed half an hour earlier so that you wake up feeling more refreshed in the morning. You may decide to get off the bus a couple of stops earlier so that you can get some regular exercise. You may decide that when you get home from work, you will switch off your mobile phone and have ten to fifteen minutes of "me" time, doing something you find relaxing, or you may decide you are going to just do nothing for a few minutes to allow your head some free-thinking space.

For bigger decisions, you realise that you cannot carry out these actions by yourself. We need the assistance of others. When I had my emotional breakdown, I got a lot of support from my therapist. I was feeling so low that I didn't want to let my close family or friends know the full truth of what was happening. Deep inside, I felt like I was to blame and if they knew the truth, they may treat me in a different way. I now know that although these thoughts were irrational, they are common with individuals who find themselves in a similar situation. If this is you, I recommend that you get some professional help.

So the next step of the five-step strategy is **Team**. Who is in your team? Who do you go to when you need help, personally or professionally? Your situation and what you decide you want to change will impact who you choose to be in your team. You will not just have one team, but several teams, depending on the decisions you make and the various roles you have in your life.

I used to be a very independent person. I still am independent, but I have learnt it's a strength and not a weakness to ask for assistance from others. Just like the human body is made up of different organs, each of which has a specific function to carry out, different people are gifted with different talents. Imagine a world if we all had the same occupation and skills. No matter; even if we classify ourselves as an expert, we can all benefit from working with others.

In my new role as a business owner, I realised quite quickly I had a lot to learn. The more I learnt, the more I realised that the tasks that needed to be done were too much for me. I got myself several coaches to help with the various aspects of my business. The coaches had their own areas of expertise, and I was able to learn a lot of new information and skills in a short space of time. I have included some of that learning in subsequent chapters of this book. I also learnt the difference between the words "group" and "team." I learnt that if I was a member of a team, Together, Everyone Achieves More. Even with my coaches, we were learning from each other.

So now you have seen the benefits and the characteristics of a good team player, how would you rate yourself?

On a scale of 0 to 10, how would you rate yourself? 0 is "I am an ineffective member of a team," and 10 is "I am an effective member of all of the teams that I am in." _____

If you scored low, what are some things that you can do to start to improve? If you scored high, what are some things that you can still improve on to make you an even better team player? Remember: Your goal is to be a good team player and not just be a member of a group.

As I carried out the various actions above and worked with my therapist, I found out I had a few dormant emotions that were impacting my decision-making skills. They were subconsciously making me behave like a passive learner. My therapist asked me a question that impacted me in a remarkable way; she asked, ***"Ruth, who do you allow to help you?"***

On the surface, this question may seem odd, but she had realised in the hour or so she had spoken with me that I only allowed people to know what I wanted them to know. Even with close friends and family, I was not always honest about my feelings. However, this has changed. It did not happen straight away, but one step at a time. As I run my seminars, or as I am now doing in this book, I realised that sharing my experiences, in an honest and open way, impacted the lives of others in a positive way. The people I worked with one-to-one or in small groups became motivated, and they soon realised they had the skills within them to make beneficial changes in their lives. I want you to decide to do something positive to benefit yourself (or someone very important to you).

After reading my personal reflection, you are probably now feeling some emotions, either positive or negative ones. I found my own emotions had been affecting my mindset and making me inactive, subconsciously, in some areas of my life, especially after I was made redundant. Although working in a challenging school was difficult, I had an identity and a sense of purpose. Each day I went to work, I knew that I was making a difference. Losing my job as a deputy head teacher had taken away my identity and my purpose. This was a deep revelation, I learnt.

So the third step in my five-step strategy is **Emotions**. What emotions do you think I was feeling as I wrote the above? What emotions are you feeling now about the situation I shared? What emotions are you feeling now about your own situation? Now would be a good time to stop reading and reflect on what is going on internally in your body. I know as I type, I am reconnecting again with some deep emotions I thought I had buried, and I can feel my stomach churning. You may be feeling something similar or your own reaction to emotions; however, your body reacts, take a mental note. Next time you feel that way, you may want to explore why.

As I worked with my therapist and discussed some really painful situations, I realised that my emotions started to change. Instead of things being a burden, they felt a lot lighter. I found using the skills of honest talking and active listening, by both the therapist and myself, resulted in significant changes in my life.

What are some emotions that you are feeling now? Are you feeling brave enough, now (not some time in the future), to start to take action?

I hope that you have answered yes to the last question, because doing something positive is step 4. The fourth step in my five-step strategy is **Positivity.**

After spending two months at home, following my emotional breakdown, I made the brave decision to return to work. It would have been easier for me to stay home and not return to the school. I had a medical excuse as well as an emotional reason not to return. I spoke with the head teacher's PA at the start of the week and told her about my decision to return to work; she informed me I could change my mind when the actual morning arrived. That Friday morning, I anxiously dressed for work. I did not know what to expect. I had been in education for a long time, so I knew there were a lot of stories circulating amongst the students as to why I was not in school. Even the staff would have their own version of events as to what had happened.

17

I arrived at school and parked near my classroom. I signed in at the office and let the head teacher's PA know I was on-site. I went to see key staff in my department, who were pleased to see me; that reduced the anxiety I was feeling. I learned I was going to have new classes, which was even more of a relief. That day, I saw some of the students who had behaved unacceptably in my classroom. Even though internally emotions surfaced, I did not let them know how I was feeling. When the day finally ended, I realised that I was a lot stronger than I thought. This confidence allowed me to return on Monday, and I completed the rest of the term.

I went back with a more positive mindset because I knew why I was returning. I wanted closure to the incident that had happened. For closure to happen, I had to confront the very thing that had caused me pain and anxiety. I had to go back and overcome the deep emotional pain I was feeling. I wanted to be a positive role model to both my colleagues and the students at school. I wanted to show them that even though I was demotivated months earlier, I was now returning to work motivated. You may not be strong enough to make the same decisions I made, but I knew, personally, it was the right thing to do. You need to make your own decisions, personally.

I spoke with my colleagues and staff; I had become a positive role model to them. I was able to work with members of my immediate department and the students to develop and carry out actions that would increase the department's results in the forthcoming GCSE and BTEC examinations. As we worked together, we started to see things which had been challenges before being solved, and solved more quickly. This leads me into step 5. The final step in my five-step strategy is **Success**.

What does the word "success" mean to you? The word "success" will mean different things to different people, according to their own personal experiences. For me, it's a verb and not a noun. Success for me describes a journey rather than a destination. It's a process of events that happened in my life and the subsequent choices I made. There have also been specific achievements in my life where I will say I have been successful, like when I passed my NPQH and earned my master's in education.

If you reflect on your past, you can list several things you were successful in. By the end of this chapter, I am hoping that you will be able to add other things to your list because you have become motivated to take action.

Just like in the previous chapter, I have included activities and tasks for you to complete to apply these five steps to your own personal challenges. You have seen how I used them personally in my own situation; you can do the same. I would like you to have success in reaching your own personal and professional goals.

In order to maximise your learning process, I would recommend that the steps be used in the order outlined. This will allow you to review, What changes you would like to make in your life right now? Who do you need to work with to help you make these changes? What emotions do you have about what you are currently facing?, What positive actions do you need to take right now?, and finally, What new things have you succeeded in completing? At the moment, this is a learning task. Later on in this chapter, you will be able to answer these questions in more detail and record your responses in a series of exercises.

I have used these same five steps in other areas of my personal and professional life. I am now more conscious about having a better work-life balance, and I use these same five steps with many decisions I make in my life. It's good to use a simple but effective strategy.

If you haven't already set yourself a goal, now would be a good time, before you start applying these steps to your own situation.

Think of your own challenging situation you are currently facing, be it personal, professional, or both. It's not always easy to pinpoint our challenges, so to assist you, I want you to make a list of things that are currently happening in your life or have affected you in the past. Space for your answers to this question is on page **21**. The main point of this exercise is for you to go through the process of selecting something specific you would like to improve. As you reflect, it may be easy for you to identify this challenge you are facing. You could be dealing with sickness, a loss of some kind, been made redundant, or have to relocate. However, you may not have a specific issue, but you know deep down there are some changes you want to make but cannot give them a name at present. You just know something doesn't feel right.

Let me illustrate this with a practical example. As I previously stated, I trained as a counsellor. On many occasions, a client would attend for their initial session. They would talk generally about their family and about things which were happening at home or work that was causing them problems. They would make a statement like, "Nobody seems to understand me. I spend all day doing a job I don't like to make sure that the bills are paid. When I get home, I don't get any thanks from anyone. All they seem to do is complain because I forgot to put out the rubbish out for collection in the morning."

In counselling terms, we call this the "presenting problem." However, during the session, as I asked more questions and got them to clarify what they were actually feeling and saying to us, I eventually realised that their problems were due to another issue. This issue could be low self-esteem. As they delved deeper into their feelings, they realised they were never praised as a child and were always told that they could do better at school. They realised that as they communicate with their family and friends, these same emotions surfaced. They felt no matter how hard they tried, their best was never good enough. This, in counselling terms, is called the "underlying problem," and it's this problem we would further explore in subsequent sessions so the client could see things more clearly.

As you spend time reflecting on your current situation, you too may discover more depth than you originally thought. The remainder of this book has been written in a way so you too, like the clients I worked with in person, can gain greater depth to your own personal goals you have chosen to work on.

I hope you too may identify new insights that are inter-related. As you go through this process and complete the tasks in this book, I hope you will also gain greater insight into yourself and will get to know yourself in a new or different way. The main focus of this chapter is that you are open-minded to the use of the five-step strategy to your own identified goals.

Consider these questions to help you decide your goals:

- How can I have a better work-life balance?
- How can I have a better relationship with my teenage children?
- How can I be happier in my relationship with my partner?
- How can I use my skills to impact the lives of others more?

Application Exercises

In the space below, make a list of things that are currently happening in your life or have happened to you in the past.

Things I am currently facing	Things that have happened to me in the past

From your list above, now select one or two areas you would like to explore using the five-step strategy. You have taken the first step: **Start**.

Areas:

_____

_____

When events happen in your life, you usually focus on the effects of the event instead of its causes. If you want to increase your level of motivation, it's essential that you focus on the cause of your situation and not only the effects.

When I had my emotional breakdown at work, I could have focussed on the effects of what had happened and how I was feeling angry and unmotivated. However, I took time to find out the root causes of my feelings, and that is when my breakthrough came. It resulted in me setting up my own company, Listening to Your Voice Ltd., which allowed me to know my new purpose in life, allowed me to grow and maximise my potential, but also allowed me to impact the lives of others. As I shared my experiences with others, I was given a new role. They started to call me an inspirational well-being coach. They realised I was using my painful experiences in a positive way, which was an encouragement to others. I could have been bitter. I could have decided to take my school to a tribunal. I could have harmed myself or turn to other self-destructive habits. Instead, I made the choice that I would use my experiences to help others.

In this new role, it was essential that I had people to help me, as I was moving out of my comfort zone and into my stretch zone. I have a variety of coaches and mentors to help me with the new opportunities that have arisen. These coaches use their expertise and knowledge to assist me, but I also have a part to play. I have to apply what they are teaching me to my own personal situation. If I don't do my part, then I will not get the results I expect. If I only apply what they have taught me half-heartedly, then my results will be half-hearted as well. The saying is true, "You reap what you sow." From a scientific or a garden's point of view, it should really say, "You reap more than you sow." You put into the ground one kernel of corn but you reap several ears of corn.

The next step that we looked at was **Team.** Who is in your team? Remember that the word team stands for "Together, Everyone Achieves More."

_____

_____

_____

_____

The third step was **Emotions**. How are you feeling, after completing the first couple of exercises? Write your positive and negative feelings in the relevant column in the table.

Positive Feelings	**Negative Feelings**

When you are going through challenges in our lives, you can feel demotivated and dwell on negative feelings instead of positive ones. When you are feeling low, it's essential you have something you can reflect on that reminds you about your achievements of the past. Isn't that why we display our graduation picture or other pictures in our homes? Isn't that why we display certain qualifications in our offices at work?

I want you now to do something positive, which is step four, **Positivity**. Make a list of at least ten things you have achieved in your life, from childhood. As you go through this process, it will give you the opportunity to recall and to celebrate the small and large achievements of your past (some of which you may have forgotten you had achieved).

When you are feeling low, it's essential you know you have had successful times in your past; the emotions you are currently feeling are due to a lack of focus and or some other external factor, as shown in Maslow's Hierarchy of Needs, discussed in the last chapter. If these low feelings persist, then you need to go and see your doctor or other health professional and receive relevant professional treatment. I had group and individual therapy, and even though it was hard, it equipped me with skills needed to help me in different areas of my life. It made me put the event which had happened in school into context and to realise my response was normal to what I had gone through.

What are some of your achievements? Write them in the table below.

Achievements			
1		6	
2		7	
3		8	
4		9	
5		10	

Your final task is to use these strategies and set at least two goals you want to achieve while you read the next section of the book, **"The Importance of Taking Action."** These will be your success criteria. When you complete reading this book, you will be able to evaluate if you have been successful in reaching your own personal goals. I want you to be able to confidently say you have taken the final step and achieved **Success**.

Personal Goals	
1	
2	
3	
4	

If you have completed all of the exercises above, then you have used the technique of accelerated learning; you are now an active learner. Your level of commitment to improving your motivation will have also increased.

On a scale from 0 to 10, where 0 is you are feeling totally demotivated and 10 is you are highly motivated, how do you now score? _____

If you are still not sure if this strategy is for you, I would like you to continue reading this book with an open mind, as I will be sharing case studies and practical examples of individuals who have used these same steps. As you read, I hope your confidence will increase so you know it's also possible for you to achieve your own goals.

The next section of the book will focus on the importance of taking action to complete the goals you have set above. It will assist you in achieving better outcomes when you are given the same opportunities as other people.

Summary

In this chapter, we have learnt the following:

- The theoretic process of the five-step strategy,
- How you can apply S.T.E.P.S. to your own personal or professional challenges, and
- Why it's important to be an active learner and put this strategy in place to motivate yourself.

Action Points

- Complete the exercises in this chapter, if you have not answered them already.
- Find a picture of someone you admire as a role model and list his or her positive qualities. You will find that that you would like to possess these same qualities in your own life.
- Visualise what success would look like for you; write your own definition of the word "success." Copy the definition onto several cards and place them in key places to remind you of your goal.

Section 2
THE IMPORTANCE OF TAKING ACTION

In chapter 1, we discussed what motivation is and why it's important that you know the things you can do to motivate yourself in your personal and professional lives. In the last chapter, you were introduced to the five-step strategy, which you can use to motivate yourself to learn how to take action when new opportunities are within your reach. You also used the strategy of accelerated learning (if you completed the exercises at the end of the chapter).

Before we move to the next section of taking action, let me summarise the five steps you can take when you want to be motivated to learn.

1. **Start**. Once you have identified where you currently are and the goals you want to achieve, you need to take a step, in any direction. If you do not move, you will be standing still and not making any progress towards your goals.

2. **Team**. Surround yourself with others who will build you up. Remember: Team stands for Together, Everyone Achieves More.

3. **Emotions**. Give a name to the negative and positive emotions you feel. If you need help, reach out and get some assistance. When I was having my emotional meltdown at school, I should have told someone I was feeling angry, instead of burying that emotion and saying I was feeling fine, which was not the truth. As I write, I am using the help of a trained therapist and also a couple of trained coaches, who are helping me to develop my business in their areas of expertise. I have learnt that good coaches have a coach to develop them to be excellent coaches. Learning never stops.

4. **Positivity.** Each day, spend some time doing something positive towards your goal or to assist others in reaching their goals.

5. **Success.** Keep a journal or diary where you record the goals you are achieving daily, weekly, and monthly. As you read over the entries, you will be able to see your own personal journey to success. You too will be able to conclude that success is a journey and not a destination.

When I ran my first seminar, one woman decided that she was going to take action. After the meeting, she told me she wanted to have coaching sessions with me on a regular basis. We completed the necessary contract, and the sessions began. She always arrived early for her session. As the coaching commenced, she would go through each of the exercises needed to support each of the five steps above. At the end of the session, she achieved her initial goals and much more. When we looked at the report from her Motivation Map, she had a high level of motivation. She completed her coaching sessions and has put the strategies learnt into practice. She is also in the process of setting up her own business to use her skills.

Another woman who attended the seminar decided to have coaching sessions. However, she did not confirm a start date when I called her. I contacted her again, but she delayed working with me. I am sure that if I was to contact her again, I would get a similar response, unless she has become motivated to take action.

Which individual do you identify with? Have you completed the action points from the end of chapter 2, or are you putting them off for tomorrow? Remember, tomorrow never comes.

Are you motivated to learn? Do you want to have a positive outcome when opportunities arise? Will you be prepared to step into your new roles?

As you will discover as you read section 2 of this book, I took action when opportunities became available. As I am writing this chapter, one of the opportunities I took when it became available was to attend the London Business Show in December 2015; I also participated in speed networking with 4 Networking. At the end of my session, as I was preparing to leave, I was asked to share my business with a gentleman who was waiting for the next session, and I did. He was impressed with my business ideas and how I wanted to use my experiences to support others who were having challenges in their life.

The following week, we met for a chat and a drink. Two weeks later, I was introduced to one of his colleagues, who hired me as a presenter on a new community TV programme, *The Great British Good News Show*. One of the aims of the show is to share more good news items in the media. At the time of writing this book, I have filmed the first six episodes. We have currently started a new show called *Modern Britain Today*. What would have happened if I did not take action when these opportunities came my way? As a member of 4Networking.biz, I have been able to meet other business owners who have helped me to grow my business.

As a result of these opportunities, I was asked to share my experiences on what is called a "4 Sight," where business owners share insights into themselves or describe how they can help other business owners. At the time of writing I have shared the following topics,

- Five steps to motivate you to take action,
- Say yes to new opportunities, and
- Well-being as a business owner.

What would have happened if I did not take the necessary actions when these opportunities arose? I wouldn't be writing about them now.

I took another opportunity and joined Your Business Community (YBC), a support group for small businesses. I have exhibited with them several times, including at the London Business Show in May and November 2016, along with other bigger established businesses, on YBC Street. A year ago, I would have never thought this could be possible when I first attended the show in December 2015.

When I exhibited at the Hammersmith and Fulham Means Business Show, I was introduced to the London Healthy Workplace Charter. This charter is an award, which can be used on marketing documents to show the business looks at the well-being of their staff in eight key areas. Additional information about this charter, including a website link for the national charter as well as the London based one, is found at the end of this book. I have incorporated work around this charter into my business model, including being trained as a verifier with the Mayor of London.

From these three experiences, I have been able to show you the impact of decisions that I took. What opportunities are you going to miss if you do not prepare yourself to take action? In this section, I will share a number of strategies that you can use while taking action.

In chapter 2, I shared with you the acronym S.T.E.P.S. to help you learn how you can get started towards achieving your goal. In section 2, I am going to share another acronym: L.E.A.R.N. This is the practical application of the how the five-step strategy can be applied to the goals you identified in the last chapter.

What Is L.E.A.R.N.?

I have been a teacher for over twenty-five years, and assisting both students and staff with learning has been an integral part of my role. What do I mean by the word L.E.A.R.N. in the context of this book?

L. The ability to **Listen Effectively**. In the next chapter, you will learn how to be an active listener and not a passive listener.

E. The ability to **Engage**. In chapter 4, how to engage in the process and the role our attitudes and behaviour play in achieving our goals.

A. The right **Attitude**. In chapter 5, you will be asked the question, "Do I have the right attitude?"

R. How to **Reflect** and make our own choices about actions we will take. In chapter 6, you have to decide if you are going to follow the crowd or be different. Are you going to be in the majority or the minority?

N. What **New Steps** do you want to work on achieving in the future. Chapter 7 allows you to monitor your progress as you have read this book. It allows you to evaluate what steps have you taken and what next steps you will have to take to reach your goals.

As I completed my master's, I discovered that our level of learning impacts our outcomes. There are three modes of learning: shallow, deep, and profound.

Shallow learning is superficial. It's just like the surface of an iceberg or a plant with weak roots. This type of learning is done by the majority of individuals as they remain within their comfort zones.

Deep learning, by contrast, is below the surface of the iceberg. If you use the growth of a plant as an example, the roots have been established. People who use deep learning will stretch themselves outside of their comfort zone. They will apply the knowledge they have gained in their own way, to their own situations. Others observing them will see growth.

Profound learning takes time. It gets to the core of the situation. You will go into your pain zone if it will help achieve your goal. You will naturally apply what you have learnt to a variety of situations. You will be in the minority group and stand out from the crowd. Your growth will be noticeable by all you come in contact with. Profound learning uses both S.T.E.P.S. and L.E.A.R.N. together to make the most of opportunities when they arise.

My goal for you, as you read this next section, is you will become either a deep or profound learner, if you are not there already.

Chapter 3

LISTENING EFFECTIVELY

In this chapter, you are going to be introduced to the first part of L.E.A.R.N.: "Listening Effectively." In chapters 1 and 2, we looked in detail about the different characteristics between active and passive learners. I hope you have chosen to be an active learner. In this chapter, you are going to learn the difference between active and passive listening; with these skills, you can listen more effectively when you are having conversations with others.

What Is listening?

Listening is an active process. It involves the use of many of your senses, not just hearing (the obvious one). Listening involves the interaction of many things taking place simultaneously, which allows you to accurately receive and understand the messages which are being relayed by another person.

Scenario One: The Board Meeting

You are in a meeting with colleagues and evaluating the impact of a new strategy that has been introduced. As you sit around the board table, you notice only some of the people are taking part in the discussions. They are evaluating their ideas using a SWOT analysis. This is a tool that identifies an issue's strengths, weaknesses, opportunities, and threats. Although others are present in the meeting, their minds appear to be elsewhere. When they are asked a question, they have to ask for it to be repeated – not just once, but every time they are addressed.

Scenario Two: At Home

You arrive home from work. You want to discuss some developments that happened at the office, but as you talk with your partner, you can sense he or she is distant, so you abandon the conversation and do something else instead. Inside, you have a lot of negative emotions, but you do not share them because you don't want to have an argument and further increase your stress level.

Signs of a Good Listener

Did you ever have a conversation with another person and felt you were not being listened to?

When you are engaged in a conversation, you not only listen to the words that are being said, you also look for changes in body language. Are they nodding their head as you speak? Are they making a sound that shows they are listening? Are they able to clarify with you the main points of the conversation?

How effective a listener are you? Answer the questions below, honestly but quickly:

1. Do you interrupt?
2. Do you talk over them?
3. Do you finish their sentences for them?
4. Do you stop talking and listen to the other person?
5. Do you make them feel relaxed?
6. Do you put other thoughts out of your mind?
7. Do you fully concentrate on what they are saying?
8. Do you nod and use other gestures or words to encourage them to continue?
9. Do you maintain eye contact?
10. Do you avoid unnecessary interruptions?

Which statements did you answer yes to?

_____

Which statements did you answer no to?

_____

A good listener would have answered yes to questions 4–10.

I hope the exercise above would have helped you to recognise in yourself when you are not listening. You now have an honest starting point to assist you as you read the remainder of this chapter.

Active and Passive Listening

You learnt in the previous chapters how to be active learners. In this chapter, you are going to learn how to be an active listener. From the exercise above, you will now have a better understanding about how good you are at listening to others during a conversation.

Active listeners fully concentrate on the conversation that is taking place. They listen with all of their senses. They need to ensure they engage with the person talking so they can tell they are listening. This is achieved by the use of nonverbal messages, often referred to as body language. Active listeners maintain eye contact, nod their heads, and smile. If they are observed by another person, they will usually be seen to be mirroring the expressions of the speaker. This allows the person to speak more easily, honestly, and openly. A sense of trust develops between the people having the conversation.

Passive listeners, on the other hand, only use the sense of hearing. They only pick up sound vibrations. Passive listeners just absorb the information and record what has been said. The majority of what is being said may not be interpreted as the speaker intended. As the conversation is taking place, they may be seen looking at their watch, a clock, or another item in the room. They shuffle papers or doodle on a pad. They look bored or uninterested. They try to second-guess where the speaker is going, and when the conversation is finished, they are in a rush to leave.

The prose below summarises these main points. After I interact with a client, I present them with a copy as a gift, to remind them of the importance of listening.

Listening to Your Voice

How many of us actually listen to the person we are having a conversation with? Really listen? Not just to the actual words that they are saying but also to the hidden language that is often referred to as body language.

Listening. This is an active process. It involves the use of many of our senses, not just hearing, the obvious one. What tone of voice are they using? What expressions are on their face? What are the surroundings like in which the conversation is taking place? Is it a place of peace or a place of conflict? How many individuals are in the room? Is the conversation in person or taking place virtually? What are the ages of the individuals? What is the relationship like between the individuals or the group who are talking? All of these factors and many others will affect the conversation.

Listening to ... The conversation must have a goal, a purpose, for the meeting to occur. Do you know what the agenda is? Is it a spontaneous conversation? Your physical body may be in the location where you are having the conversation, but where is your mind? To really listen, the mind and the body must be both present in the same location.

Listening to your ... Now this is the core of the conversation. You need to listen to someone else. You need to have a dialogue and not a monologue. Too often, you are not really listening to the other person but formulating our own ideas in our mind. Listening is an unselfish act, as you are putting the needs of another person above our own. You are letting them know that they truly matter, that you value their time and ideas, which they are sharing with you. In an ideal situation, you will both benefit from the conversation.

Listening to your voice. When you think about these words, you automatically think about the vocal voice. What about the unspoken voice? Communication takes place between individuals with looks, gestures, and specific habits. Sign language, body language, and other forms of communication all have a voice.

As you interact with others today, really listen to their voice. It may be the still voice that guides your daily activities; it may be interactions with family members, colleagues at work, other learners, even a total stranger. Who you are conversing with is important, but what is even more important is that you actively listen to their voice and what they are actually saying to you. Then ask yourself, have you totally understood their message?

Really listening to others is not easy at first, but with practice, you will have a richer life and more fulfilling relationships. Go on, give it a try. You will notice the difference. You will feel so much better when the conversation is finished.

After reading the prose, I want you to honestly ask yourself the question, *"How effective am I as a listener? What actions do I need to take to become a better active listener?"*

At first, it may be hard to put all of these steps in place, but with practice, it will get easier. When I trained to be a counsellor, we did an exercise that brought home the differences between the two types of listeners. We worked in pairs. One of us was A and the other B. The first time we spoke, we both talked about our own topic for two minutes; we were not allowed to engage with each other. The next time, A spoke but B had to do whatever it took to not listen to them: walk away, put their fingers in their ears, turn their back, and so on. The third time, A spoke and B listened actively, using effective body language as discussed above. After the exercise was finished, we discussed how we felt in each role. If you have someone near, it would be good to give this exercise a try so you can see what it's like in each of the situations. As you can imagine, we didn't like to be ignored, so we felt relieved when we could communicate effectively with each other.

This exercise taught us the following methods to improve our listening skills:

1. Make eye contact.

2.   Make the other person feel relaxed. Smile.
3.   Show other signs of affirmation, like nodding your head.
4.   Know the reason why the conversation is taking place.
5.   Have both your body and mind in the same room.
6.   Have a dialogue and not a monologue.
7.   Put the needs of the other person above your own needs.
8.   Avoid distracting actions; don't look at your watch.
9.   Don't look bored.
10. Ask questions that clarify the main points of the conversation.
11. Paraphrase what has been said by using sentences like, "Do you mean ...?"
12. Make the shift between the roles of speaker and listener as smooth as you can.

Some Barriers to Active Listening

Even by adopting the majority of the suggestions above into your conversations, there may still be some barriers in a conversation.

- I am sure that you have experienced speaking with someone when they are having two conversations at once. You too may be guilty of this. You may be on the phone with one person and at the same time have a conversation with someone in the room with you.
- You may be distracted by external noises due to the environment you are in, or the TV, radio, or computer in the background.
- You may not agree with what they are saying, and internally you are having another conversation in your head.
- You may not be feeling well; you may be tired, hungry, or thirsty; or you may even need the toilet.
- You may be bored, because you have heard the same conversations several times before.
- They may talk in a monotone, and you may find it hard to concentrate on what they are saying.
- You may be preoccupied with personal issues which are causing you stress.
- You may have a closed mind and therefore don't want to listen to other views.

What Happens if You Become an Active Listener?

Let's return to the two scenarios at the start of this chapter and see how they could be improved using the skills you learnt above.

Scenario One: The Board Meeting

Prior to the meeting, everyone was given a copy of the agenda and a copy of the report which was being discussed. The agenda listed the name of the person presenting each item. All members of the board were expected to take part in the SWOT analysis and share in the discussion. At key times in the meeting, the chair would choose one of the members of the board to clarify what had been discussed, and the main points would be recorded on a flip chart for further review. The minutes of the meeting would be circulated afterwards, and further recommendations would be reported back by email by a given date.

If the meeting were held this way, there would more engagement by all attendees, before, during, and after the meeting. Everyone would feel their contributions were valuable and the meeting was worthwhile.

Scenario Two: At Home

Your partner arrived home from work, exhausted. She had a difficult day with a series of long meetings that drained all her energy. She just needs some time to relax and unwind. Instead of having a conversation straight away, you allow her space so she can enjoy being at home. Previously, you each agreed to share what happened at work for a short period, and for the rest of the evening, you enjoy each other's company without speaking about anything work related.

If these practices were done on a regular basis, the outcome would be less stress and better communication between you and your partner. You would have put into place some of the skills needed to be an active listener.

Summary

In this chapter, we have learnt the following:

- What's the difference between active and passive listening?
- How to evaluate how good a listener you are by answering a series of questions.
- How to have your body and mind in the same place.
- Active listening involves the use of all five senses, but passive listening only uses the sense of hearing.
- Some of the barriers to active listening.
- The signs of a good listener.

Action Points

- Choose an individual you want to have an active conversion with and consciously implement some of the strategies outlined in this chapter.
- Decide beforehand the topic of the conversation, as this will work better than making it general. (Make it someone you know well: a partner, family member, or good friend.)
- Evaluate the conversion and record "What Went Well" (**W.W.W.**) and ways that the conversation could be "Even Better If" (**E.B.I.**).
- Using the E.B.I. suggestions, have another conversation to put the strategies in place. Two key issues to improve at this time are planning and practice. The better the planning, and the more the plan is put into practice, the better the outcome will be.
- Evaluate this new conversation using W.W.W. and E.B.I.
- Repeat this process with other conversations, and with other individuals, until active listening becomes a habit.

Note: As you go through this process, you will naturally develop habits to become a more active listener. I know because it happened to me.

Chapter 4

LEVEL OF ENGAGEMENT

Introduction

Sarah and Tom have been dating for a couple of years. They have decided to take their relationship to the next level. Tom wants to make the occasion really special and arranges a meeting with Sarah's parents, to let them know what he is planning. As you can imagine, they are really happy. The day arrives for Tom to surprise Sarah. The invitations have been sent out, the venue booked, and the catering sorted. Some of Sarah's friends are arranging to take her to the hotel.

As Sarah walks into the room, she is lost for words. She sees so many people she has not seen for a while. Tom greets her with a kiss and then gets down on one knee. She smiles lovingly at him, as he takes out a jewellery box.

Tom begins, "Sarah, I cannot imagine my life without you. You have made such a difference in my life. Will you give me the pleasure of becoming my wife? Will you marry me?"

After catching her breath, Sarah responds, "Yes. Yes!"

Everyone in the room starts to applaud. The room is a happy place.

If Sarah and Tom did not have such a solid relationship and were not supported by others, this might not have been such a joyous occasion.

What happens when a business has a foundation built on solid relationships, where employees feel supported by each other? Some businesses have these values, but they are in the minority.

What happens when business owners ensure that their staff are happy and motivated?

What happens when good relationships become the core of what they do and the decisions they make?

As an individual, how can you make a difference at your workplace? It starts with you making a conscious decision that despite the actions of others, you will put these values into practice. Tom had a goal, but unless he carried out specific actions, that goal wouldn't have been achieved. Similar steps are needed to make a difference in the workplace.

What Does the Term "Engagement" Mean in a Professional Setting?

In employment circles, engagement doesn't mean employees are happy. The employees may appear to be happy, but that doesn't mean they will always work as hard as they can, or that they are working as productively as they can. Even with benefits such as free gym membership, free massages, and discounted health benefits, employees are not always engaged.

Employment engagement is the emotional commitment that the employee has to the organisation and its goals. Tom and Sarah had an emotional commitment to each other and to their goals. If they want a long and happy marriage, they will have to be committed to make the sacrifices needed for the relationship to grow.

Personally, I would say engagement in a workplace has to do with attitudes, behaviours, and outcomes. Employees with good attitudes are loyal to the company. They usually go the extra mile. We would say their behaviour is good. The outcome of this level of engagement would be fewer conflicts at work; employees would have a reduced sickness rate, and this would create higher productivity in the workplace. These are three benefits of looking after your employees as an employer; I share them with my clients when we discuss the topic of well-being in the workplace.

How Do You Know Someone Is Engaged in the Workplace?

Scenario One: The Late Phone Call

It is 5 p.m., the time when Dave is due to finish work. His boss comes into his office and tells him that management expects them to produce a key report for a meeting that is taking place tomorrow. His boss says the report is very important. What should Dave do? Should he leave work, as his contracted working hours are 9 to 5? Or should be stay and help his boss to complete the report?

What would you do if you were Dave? Would you stay in the office and help, or would you go home?

Scenario Two: The Weekly Business Meeting

It is the weekly business meeting for your company. How do you turn up for the meeting? Do you show up only because you have to there, even though you are not going to actively participate? Or do you turn up prepared, having read the documents and ready to contribute to the discussion?

These two scenarios will show you if you are engaged with your work activities or not. Even if you work for yourself, there are going to be situations when you have to decide your priorities.

This chapter will focus on you and how you carry out different tasks that are work related. Before you start this chapter, decide if you are going to have an open mind to learn. Are you going to have a negative attitude? Are you going to engage in this learning process, or are you going to skim over the chapter? How you answer these questions and your actions that follow will indicate your level of engagement in a working environment.

When You Find Yourself in a New Situation, How Do You Act?

I worked in education for over twenty-five years, but in March 2015, I started a new business, Listening to Your Voice Ltd., because I made the conscious decision that when the new school year began, I wouldn't be returning to teaching. It was a brave decision, as teaching was the only real career that I had known. Earlier in my career, I had worked as a research assistant, but after a year, I knew that I didn't want to pursue a career in research. Because of the decision I made, I knew I would have a rapid learning curve. Between the months of March and September, I completed the essentials in creating my business: name, logo, business plan. I had laid the initial foundations.

That August, I informed my family and friends I would be celebrating my birthday at the end of September, by holding my first seminar, called "Five Steps to Overcoming Challenges." This seminar used the same five steps that we discussed in chapter 2. During the month of September, I attended a workshop led by an experienced speaker, who taught me how I should organise my seminar (I have subsequently been a crew member with this same speaker on several occasions). I had already booked the venue; now I needed to arrange marketing and purchase the supplies I would need to host the event. I was now learning to be an event manager. I had the skills needed to be a successful motivational speaker, before, during, and after I put on my own events.

Let's return to the day of my first event. I arrived early at the venue, along with some friends, so we could prepare the room. Guests started to arrive about 7:15, and I started speaking at 7:30. As you can imagine, I was nervous at first and held onto my notes. As the participants began to engage in the various interactive activities, I began to relax, and before long, I was speaking without my notes. By the time that I finished speaking at 8:15, I could tell the participants appreciated my presentation. They gave me a lot of positive feedback, which made me quite proud. At the end of the presentation, two participants asked to continue working with me, one to one, as part of my personal development programme.

Another participant visited their local library to enquire if I could hold the same seminar there. After I submitted a proposal, I was able to arrange a series of seminars and personal development sessions. Plans are being made to run similar events in other venues.

Following the success of these seminars, I decided to let other companies know about my business, so in December 2015, I attended the London Business Show. This was the first time that I had attended such an event. I arrived to a hall full of exhibitors, and with no one I knew by my side, I engaged with the exhibitors. Even though I felt out of my depth, I did not let my inner fears hold me back. I attended the show again, both in May and November 2016, but this time as an exhibitor. What a difference a few months had made.

As I walked around, in December 2015, I was drawn to several exhibitions and observed what was happening. One such exhibition was for speed networking. Below is a list of the various actions that I took the first time that I participated in speed networking.

- I asked questions from the organisers about how speed networking works.
- I was then asked, "Do you want to put your name down for the next session?"

- I gave them a copy of my business card and they added me to the list. The session was due to start in an hour.
- As I walked away to visit other exhibitions, I had a decision to make: Would I return early, arrive on time, or be late for the networking session so I had an excuse not to take part?
- I turned up about ten minutes early and took a seat along with other participants.
- I took out my pile of business cards and listened as the rules were explained. I then did my first pitch.

I described my company and explained that I worked with businesses who wanted to motivate their staff and improve their engagement, tailoring a series of workshops or seminars, using the five-step strategy described in chapter 2. This strategy takes you from where you are now to a place where you have achieved your own personal, department, or company goal. I shared I have three packages, bronze, silver and gold, depending on how bespoke the services they required were.

Other services, I offered are based on my skills obtained as a licensed practitioner for Motivation Maps. I then concluded by sharing some of the benefits of working with me. I shared all this information in sixty seconds. I had to do this not once but fifteen times, to a range of different types of businesses. As you can imagine, I was very tired when I finished, but I also had a buzz. I decided that I would return to the Business Show the next day and repeat this process again. After this session, I was given information about my local group. I am now a passport member of 4N and network in various locations around London. At my local group, I have the role of visiting coordinator. Information about how you can join this networking organisation can be found in the Useful Links chapter.

These experiences taught me many things about engagement. I had to make suitable preparation. I needed to have my business cards with me. I had to carry out the behaviours expected of me as a participant. I had to explain to other business owners what services I was offering. The outcome of my excellent level of engagement was that I got several leads from other business owners. This was a great way to grow my business.

Now when I attend networking meetings, I change my pitch to be relevant to other business owners. I am learning the skills to be a great networker. Networking is both a social activity and a business opportunity.

Just like with Sarah and Tom, there had to be a time of learning about the other person before decisions were made to take the relationship to the next level. These experiences gave me the confidence to move my business to the next level. It also made me realise I was 100 percent engaged in what I was doing; 99 percent wouldn't have been good enough. I totally believed in myself, what I was doing, and the positive differences my business would make in the lives of others.

Why Is It Important that You Are Engaged in What You Do?

As I reflected on these situations, I realised I had a choice to make about my level of engagement at every stage. At the end of chapter 2, you decided on a series of goals you would like to work on as you read the remainder of this book. In chapter 3, you learnt about the importance of using active listening skills instead of being a passive listener. So once again, you have a choice to make: Are you going to be engaged in your learning?

Jake, Ellen, John, and Elizabeth were assigned to a meeting to discuss new working practices being considered at their company. Management wanted input from staff about the new practices before a final decision was made. The changes involved continuous professional development.

Scenario Three: Poor Level of Engagement

Jake and Ellen arrived at the meeting and sat next to each other. They chatted all throughout the meeting. They saw the meeting as a waste of time, as they believed that management had already decided to make the change. They reasoned the meeting was called so management could say staff had been consulted. They saw nothing wrong with attending the meeting with a poor attitude and no engagement in the procedures.

Scenario Four: Good Level of Engagement

Before John and Elizabeth arrived at the meeting, they thoroughly read the proposal document and came prepared with a series of questions they wanted management to clarify. As they engaged in the decisions that were being made, they concluded, "We have to attend this meeting as part of our roles. We are getting paid by the company, and this training will be essential for our roles. This meeting will allow us to contribute in the future."

The two scenarios above show that there is another area to the topic of engagement: personal values and beliefs. As employees, did Jake and Ellen show appropriate values? What about the two-way commitment between employers and employees?

This is not just related to your work environment. This commitment should be shown in all of our significant relationships: with friends, families, and organisations we are members of (even those we volunteer for).

What Is My Role?

Another reason why people are not fully committed, as they should be, is they do not feel part of the decision-making process. They feel decisions are being imposed on them, as in scenario three above. Children, even as young as two years old, do not like to be told what they should be doing, so as adults, we would also like to be genuinely involved. You should ask your employers about the organisation's goals and values and be committed to contribute to its success.

Let's return now to your own personal goals. If you are working on a personal goal, think about what you could do to hold yourself accountable to your goal, so you can increase your level of commitment.

You may not be aware of this, but your attitude and tone can affect the outcome of a meeting. When I first discovered this information, I had to reflect on how I showed up for meetings, especially ones that I thought were a waste of my time. I had to make some conscious changes, and you do too.

When things go wrong in a relationship, you often blame the other person, but if you are truly honest, you have a part to play too, no matter how small. I shared earlier about the emotional challenges that I went through at work. I was recently introduced to a powerful tool called the Circle of Blame. In this tool, you look at an event of your choice, in detail. You look at who was to blame for all of the decisions that were made. This may be two people or your entire organisation. I decided that I would use the tool to evaluate the events that took place which had resulted in my emotional breakdown.

The Circle of Blame

This tool evaluates the part you play in a challenging situation. This could be something from the past or something you are currently experiencing.

After you evaluate the part you played, determine what you would do differently, if you are faced with a similar situation again. This section is called "My New Learning."

Below are the results for my Circle of Blame. I call it "My Career Choice."

I Am to Blame Because:

- I did not take responsibility early enough,
- I should not have allowed the situation to continue for as long as it did,
- I should have had better feelings about myself and my own self-worth, and
- I should have challenged management because their actions prevented me from attaining the targets which were set as part of my performance review. I had agreed to stay in the school to complete a particular task, which they now wanted to postpone.

My New Learning

- Due to this incident and other events which took place, like when I was made redundant, I didn't want to put myself back into a place where I felt vulnerable and had these negative emotions.
- I now know I have a choice about how I act in a situation I find uncomfortable.
- I need to speak up earlier and use my voice in whatever way management will listen, be it the spoken voice, email, letter, or a combination of different forms of communication. I need to persist until I know they are actively listening to what I am saying.
- I have to speak up when situations are not right and not sit on the fence or stay within my comfort zone because I don't want to rock the boat.
- I have to value myself and know my own self-worth.
- I have to speak up earlier for others; in this case, the students whose grades were suffering because a minority of voices were more powerful than their one.

In the "I Am to Blame" section, you will see that there is a total lack of engagement; each point made was a negative statement. However, when you look at the "My New Learning" section, there is total engagement in the process. Each sentence is positive.

I found the exercise very liberating, as it made me stop and reflect on an incident that had caused me a lot of pain. However, now instead of focusing on the effects of what happened, I was now able to focus on the causes. From this new viewpoint, I took ownership for my part, but not the part that did not belong to me. This was a powerful shift in my mindset. I was taking back control.

For your own personal learning in this chapter, I would recommend that you complete a Circle of Blame for an event of your choice. This coaching tool should result in better clarity of the situation. A good starting point you could use would be the situation that caused you to set the goals you identified at the end of chapter 2.

I often find because of my own approach to a situation, I may be ruling myself out of the decision-making process, like in scenario three above.

It's essential I make the most of opportunities I am given. I might find the situation challenging, because I have to move out of my comfort zone and into my stretch or panic zone, but I have found even when I feel out of my depth, if I engage 100 percent in this new place, I will get the assistance I need. This happened to me time and time again in the early stages of establishing my business.

What Have You Learnt So Far?

Engagement has several parts that all work together. Engagement involves your attitudes, behaviours, outcomes, values, and beliefs about yourself.

In 2012, the Olympic Games took place in London; for the first time in history, they were held concurrently with the Paralympic Games. I was not able to attend the Olympic Games, but I attended the Invictus Games in 2014. These are an international Paralympic-style sports event for injured, sick or wounded armed service personnel.

I was fortunate to watch a game of seated volleyball between Great Britain and the United States. The atmosphere in the room was electrifying. After a close match, the Great Britain team won. While some people looking at the athletes would think they were limited in what they could achieve, they had achieved a level of expertise. The athletes did not let their disabilities limit their level of engagement. I know some able-bodied people wouldn't have the same level of engagement. The athletes demonstrated that they were powerful as individuals but more powerful as a team. Why? They were totally engaged in the game. They took control of their own individual circumstances, because they knew first-hand being unengaged could make them feel powerless.

How Can You Put This Learning into Practice?

Engagement is a two-way process: organisations must work to engage employees, who in turn have a choice about the level of engagement they offer the employer. Each reinforces the other.

How can organisations get the best out of their staff and create a more positive working environment? Motivational Map ® states that TEAM stands for **T**ogether, **E**veryone **A**chieves **M**ore. This shows that a partnership is taking place. This is different from the word "group." A group of people carry out a similar role or work in the same department. For a team to be effective and engaged, employees need to understand their motivation. Do your employees like to work as part of a group, or do they prefer to work alone on a project? Do they need to be praised? Do they need a detailed brief? Do they want to just be given the assignment and left to complete it themselves? No one way of working is better than another, but sometimes, we want to impose the way we work best on others. Good managers know which members of their team like to be micromanaged and which like to work independently. If they are managed the wrong way, it can leave them feeling totally demotivated.

There is a story about a group of animals working together: a bird, a monkey, and a fish. As you know, birds are good at flying, monkeys at climbing, and fish at swimming. The animals were asked to fly and climb and swim. However, they were expected to complete all the same tasks. What made things even worse was the monkey spent so much time to learning to swim and to fly, he was not as good a climber. His attention was placed in areas of weakness instead of areas of strength. The same was true of the other animals. Although this is just an illustration, the same thing happens in the workplace. For many employees, too much time is spent developing their weak areas instead of building up their areas of strength. It's so easy to lose sight of the fact that we all have our own gifts and talents, which we use in both of our personal and professional roles.

Let's return to the relationship of Sarah and Tom. As they started to spend more and more time together, they began to learn how to strengthen their relationship. They learnt how to cooperate with each other and use different strategies when conflict occurred.

In our own personal lives, conflict can arise not because we are deliberately trying to be difficult with another person, but because we have different ways of completing a task; in some cases, two people can approach the same task from totally opposite directions. We then get frustrated and annoyed because we cannot understand why others do not do things the same way we do.

This is often the cause for conflict in the workplace as well as in our personal lives. One individual wants to make a decision quickly, using the information available at the time, while the other wants to take time to look at alternative options. They want to research and find out what would be best in the long term and not just the short term. Eventually, they have to make a decision, which may please one or both of them.

However, stress is also created at work when staff members do not pull their weight. This can also be seen in personal relationships, if one person is always giving and the other is always taking. People who are always giving may have so many negative emotions within, but they don't know how to express them, as they also want to keep the peace. They are 100 percent engaged in what they do, whereas the other person feels that the relationship is 50:50. In this situation, a conversation would have to take place between both parties to strengthen the relationship. This is an example of when the Circle of Blame is useful.

Showing more consideration for the emotions of others can resolve or avoid a lot of stressful situations. Employees would take fewer sick days if they knew they were genuinely supported at work. They would be honest with their line manager about things happening at home. Relationships between parents and children would be more harmonious if they understood the needs of each other better by engaging in more meaningful conversations. Let me share with you another case study of one of my clients.

This is especially true when dealing with teenagers. Before their child became an adolescent, most parents were clear about their relationship: They were the parent and their son or daughter was the child. However, as the child becomes older, things change; society now views older teens as adults. Conversations change, and there is a shift in power as well as responsibility on the part of the child. These conflicts can put a strain on relationships. When relationships start to break down, a coach or mentor working with the family can help. The coach or mentor's role is to facilitate better communication between parents and their children. It allows both parties to see things from the other side. A different viewpoint is the cause of most conflict. Conflict taking place in the home can impact performance at work.

One statement that is used often during conflicts is, "It's fine about me putting in the effort and having the correct attitude and increasing my level of engagement, but if they do not, what is the point?"

When we discuss the various aspects of engagement, we also need to look at the importance of values and beliefs. As an individual, you cannot be responsible for the beliefs and values of another; ultimately, they choose how they act. However, I know from my own personal situation, if I remain true to my own values, I have more self-respect and self-belief. From this place of certainty and congruence, I have also learnt the importance of the word "we" and not "me." The next chapter will look in more detail at the difference these two words can have, as we discuss having the right attitude.

Summary

In this chapter, we have learnt the following:

- Engagement has to do with your attitudes, behaviours, and outcomes.
- Our actions can impact others; we discussed specific examples of causes and effects in different situations that are both professional and personal.
- The Circle of Blame is an effective tool for communication.
- Teamwork is important, and it helps to get the best out of people you have relationships with, both professionally and socially.
- Remaining true to your own personal values and beliefs is important.

Action Points

- Make a list of where you feel unengaged in your life and write them on the left side of a piece of paper; these could be personal or work-related. On the right-hand side, list things you can do to become more engaged.
- For at least one of the areas identified, complete a Circle of Blame. Write down what you should have done differently and your own personal learning.
- Write down specific ways you will now behave differently personally and professionally to help your own learning, so you can become better engaged when you are working with others.

Chapter 5

DO I HAVE THE RIGHT ATTITUDE?

What Does the Word "Attitude" Mean?

What do we mean when we say that someone has a good or bad attitude? According to the dictionary, "Attitude is a tendency to respond positively or negatively towards a certain idea, object, person, or situation." It continues to say that attitude "influences an individual's choice of action and responses to challenges, incentives, and rewards (together called stimuli)."

In this chapter, we will determine whether you have a positive or negative response when new situations arise.

From this definition, I realised that attitude isn't just how you respond in one situation. It's how you respond generally, over a long period of time. To understand this better, let me ask you this question: How would people generally describe you?

How Do Others Describe You?

Do they describe you as a positive or a negative person? Do you say that the glass is half-full or half-empty? Are you generally optimistic or pessimistic?

A common ice-breaking task is to have people in a meeting describe you. They may have known you for a long time, or they may have just met you. A simple method to do this is as follows: Pieces of paper are passed around the group, and on the top of each page a name is written. Starting at the bottom of the paper, the first person describes the person whose name is written on the top. Once they write their comment, they pass the paper to the next person, who repeats the task. This continues until everyone in the room has written something about all of the other people in the room. Once each paper is filled with comments, the paper is given to the person whose name is on the top.

These were the responses that were written on my paper:
Ruth is …

- beautiful with a smile that brightens the room,
- a real source of wisdom,
- caring and always thoughtful,
- charming and good hearted,
- friendly, cheerful and has a good personality,
- always encouraging you, a real blessing,
- very positive and energetic, really good company, and
- inspirational.

How do you think I felt when I read these comments? Would you say that I have a positive or negative attitude to the challenges that life can bring?

How would others describe you? Would they write specific positive things about you, or would they write bland, generic comments? We all know that people gravitate towards positive people instead of negative people. Remember the saying, "Birds of a feather flock together"? If you have the right attitude and characteristics, then others are going to want to work with you. Let me illustrate this from when I was a science teacher.

Scenario One

The students had to complete several investigations to gain practical and theoretical skills. To complete these experiments, they had to work in groups of two to four students. Some students would quickly find others to work with, but there would always be those who could not find a group to work with. Why? These students would never take part; they just wanted to copy the results of their peers. Some would be so lazy, they wanted someone else to draw their results table for them. As their teacher, I reminded the class that students needed to draw their own results table, as it be would needed for the next part of the investigation. Despite these instructions, I would always find a few students with the wrong attitude, who wouldn't be prepared for their independent work.

What Type of Team Player Are You?

Let's make it personal. How would your family and friends describe your attitude towards them? How would your colleagues at work describe you? What would your line manager say in a letter of reference? Would he or she say that you are a good team player or one who should be avoided, like the students described above?

What type of team player are you at home, with your friends, and at work? Do you have the same attitude in each situation? If someone was to observe you in different situations, would they say you have a split personality?

In the last chapter, we talked about the importance of being engaged. We learnt that our actions can impact others in both professional and personal situations. This doesn't mean you will act exactly the same way, all of the time. It does mean, however, that you have consistent things you will do in your professionally and personal relationships.

Can Your Environment Affect Your Attitude?

Let me illustrate this. I am generally a positive person, an optimist, as shown by the comments others wrote about me in the exercise above. However, when I had my emotional breakdown at work, I was feeling neither positive nor optimistic. Why was this? The environment I was in was not a positive one; it was a negative situation.

Because I was in a negative environment, my negative attitudes were dominant. In the last chapter, we looked at the Circle of Blame. After I changed my attitude, by accepting I was not to blame for the majority of the situation, I was able to adopt a more positive attitude about work. By the time I returned to work, I knew my self-worth, and I could focus on the causes of why I had the breakdown and not the effects. This experience taught me a valuable lesson about attitude. The environment you find yourself in, either personally or professionally, can affect your health and attitude in a profound way.

When positive people are in a positive environment, then their attitude will be generally positive. However, when positive people are in a persistently negative environment, unless they have a lot of internal strength, their attitude will change. When negative people are in a negative environment, they will rarely have a positive attitude, as their default would be to have a negative attitude.

How Do You Act when You Find Yourself in a New Environment?

When you find yourself in a new environment, what are some steps you can take so you can have a positive attitude?

As previously discussed, our attitude is influenced by our choices. It's also influenced by our surroundings and by how challenged we feel. Other factors that influence attitude include incentives and rewards. I would also like to add that our motivation for being in a new environment will affect our attitude. If you are motivated to be at the meeting, then your attitude will be more positive, compared to if you are not really motivated to attend; remember the attitudes of Jake, Ellen, John, and Elizabeth in the previous chapter.

If you have a low level of motivation, it's going to impact your attitude. However, if you have a high level of motivation, those around you will be able to see and hear that you have a positive attitude.

The Importance of We over Me

Here is another fundamental question that you need to ask when discussing attitude: Are you going to think more about your own personal needs or the needs of the team? Are you going to consider what decision(s) would be best for your family? Are you going to consider how your decisions will affect your friends?

We are going deep now, as we consider how our attitude can impact the lives of those we care about. I know personally the first time that I considered how my attitudes were affecting others, it made me think deeply. I wasn't doing anything to hurt them directly. I always like to help others, but whenever they wanted to return the favour, I always wanted to act independently. I was thinking more about my need to be independent instead of the satisfaction my friends would have when they helped me.

I have changed now as I realised asking for help did not mean I was a weak person, but actually it meant I was stronger. Remember the saying "A cord of three strands is not easily broken?" Even if we don't want to admit it, we are all dependent on others, every day of our lives. We might think we are independent, but we still need to work with others at home, at work, in our neighbourhood and as members of society.

What Are the Benefits of Having the Right Attitude?

A positive attitude can lead you to be more successful with reaching your goals. It can help you to feel happier within yourself. It can make you more optimistic about life, especially when unexpected challenges occur. You tend to worry less. In some situations, it can help you to see changes in a constructive way. Instead of seeing redundancy as a negative thing, you can see it as an opportunity to have a new job, doing something which makes you happier, with a greater sense of purpose. I now know if I had not been made redundant, and if I did not have my emotional meltdown, this book would never have been written. I wouldn't have had the numerous opportunities described in this book. I have been able to turn negative experiences into positive ones. You can choose to do the same.

How Do We Know if Someone Has a Positive Attitude?

As you observe someone who has a positive attitude, you will see them smiling more, and they will have a happier look on their face. The tone of their conversations will be a lot lighter and jollier. They walk taller, with their head held high. If they do not have to wear a uniform, you will see that they will dress in brighter colours and are proud of their appearance. There is something different about them, and you want to be in their company. They give out a lot of positive energy. If an obstacle comes in their path, instead of seeing it as a problem, they look for alternative ways to solve the problem: going around or even through. They have a high self-esteem, and you could tell they are very confident.

The title of this book is *Say Yes to New Opportunities*. When opportunities come your way because of your positive energy, you will either find a solution within yourself or find people to help you achieve your goals.

Review

If you were to carry out an audit and give yourself a score for 0 to 10, how would you score the five questions below? For these questions, 0 means that you have a low level and 10 means that you have a high level, for each of the areas given:

1. How positive is your thinking? _____
2. How motivated are you to take action? _____

3. How good a team player are you? _____
4. What is your energy level? _____
5. How happy are you? _____

How did you score? Did you get over 25 points? If you scored 30 or more, you can say that you're feeling more positive than negative. if you obtained a high score, what are some things that you can do to maintain this score?

```
┌─────────────────────────────────────────────────────────────┐
│                                                             │
│                                                             │
│                                                             │
│                                                             │
│                                                             │
└─────────────────────────────────────────────────────────────┘
```

If you got a score of less than 20, what are some things you can do to increase your score?

```
┌─────────────────────────────────────────────────────────────┐
│                                                             │
│                                                             │
│                                                             │
│                                                             │
│                                                             │
└─────────────────────────────────────────────────────────────┘
```

We have reached a pivotal moment in the book. You have to make an important decision. You have to evaluate your own attitude to your learning.

You have seen the benefits to having the right attitude in your personal and professional life, but you now need to decide which attitude you adopt.

In the past, you may have had an attitude that was in the middle of the road, neither negative nor positive. As the saying goes, you were sitting on the fence, or in the case of a drink, you were lukewarm: neither hot nor cold.

You now need to decide. Do you want to have a positive attitude? Which side of the fence do you want to be on? Do you want to be a hot drink or a cold drink?

Sometimes, you can have negative attitudes because you are tired, exhausted, or hungry, or some other need is not being met. You may not have had enough sleep, if you were awake at night caring for a young child, or you may not be eating well because you are working too late at the office. As you reflect, think about the quality of your life as a whole. We are going to look at seven areas that can impact your life, in a positive or negative way:

1. Diet
2. Exercise
3. Water
4. Fresh Air
5. Sleep
6. Relaxation
7. Relationships

Which of the areas listed above do you think you need to improve, so that you have a more positive attitude? Circle them.

Below are my own personal thoughts, as I took some time out to reflect how each of the seven areas was impacting my life.

1. I needed to ensure that I had a more balanced **diet.** I needed to eat foods which would give me more energy sustained over a longer period of time, instead of one that had my energy levels fluctuating during the day. This would also mean that I could not keep snacking and would eat meals at a more regular time.

2. I realised that I was not getting enough **exercise**. Whenever I exercised, I felt more energised and had a better mental attitude towards challenges that arose during the day. Just going for a swim boosted my energy and helped me to concentrate better.

3. I was not drinking enough **water,** and this left my body dehydrated. To help me know how much water I was drinking each day, I kept a tally chart on my fridge door. When the numbers were low, I would drink at least one glass of water. I got into a good habit of hydrating my body. I now find if I haven't had enough to drink, my body has a way of letting me know.

4. I try to get some **fresh air** each day. When I sit indoors all day, I find my level of concentration decreases in the afternoon. If I go out and get some fresh air, I am vitalised and come back and finish

my work more quickly and more accurately. It was also important as I took in the fresh air that I also make sure I took regular deep breaths to get oxygen deep into my lungs. I exhaled as deep as I could to clear the carbon dioxide out of my lungs.

5. As I improved in the four points listed above, I noticed the quality of my **sleep** also improved. At the end of the day, my body and mind were tired. After a good night's sleep, I found that I awoke in the morning with a clearer mind, ready to face the activities for the day ahead.

6. Learning to **relax** was one of my biggest challenges. I always felt that I had to be busy doing something. Part of this was due to the fact that in work, we rarely had a moment to ourselves, unless we made the time. We were always multitasking, as deadlines would be short and frequent. However, I found that if I switch off and do something I like doing (cooking, listening to music, colouring in a picture, or completing a jigsaw puzzle), when I got back to work, I was more focused on the task and completed it in less time than when I did not take a break.

7. **Good relationships** have helped me this last year, as I have made several transitions in my life. Good relationships definitely helped me to grow my business. As I attend networking events, I look forward to socialising with others. We talk about what's happening in our personal lives as well as in our businesses. This bond grows stronger the more time we spend together. We are also developing trust with each other, which is essential if you are going to be working with each other in business or recommending them to someone you know.

This would be a good time for you to take a break from reading and take some time for self-reflection. With your busy life, with all of the various activities you are engaged in, and with your constant accessibility due to the use of smartphones, iPads, and tablets, you sometimes forget to take time out to reflect on the quality of your life and your relationships. If you were to reflect on the seven areas above, how would you describe them in your own words? List your thoughts in the table below.

Area	Personal Review
Diet	
Exercise	
Water	
Fresh Air	
Sleep	
Relaxation	
Relationships	

How Can You Apply What You Have Learnt So Far?

You have learnt that attitude is about how much you focus, your mindset, whether you have positive or negative energy, and whether you are an optimist or a pessimist. The next part of this chapter will look at attitudes that are used in the workplace. These are summarised as the five Es: Enthusiasm, Efficient, Excellent, Early, Enjoyable. These attitudes are relevant not just in the workplace but also in your personal life.

1. Enthusiasm.

How enthusiastic are you about achieving the goals you set at the end of chapter 2? Do you get up each morning and have a clear plan of tasks you need to complete, or do you allow each day to go by without any sense of direction? Do you get out of bed quickly or do you drag your feet?

When I get up, I am enthusiastic, as I know I have another day to work towards my goals. This has not always been the case. My attitude towards my work has become more positive; this positivity has given me more enthusiasm.

2. Efficient

How efficient are you, whether you are working alone or as part of a team? When we are talking about efficiency, we are thinking about how little time you waste when you are actually completing a task. Do you constantly go over your work, time and time again, because you want it to be perfect? Don't get me wrong; it's important you make sure your work is presentable and the best it can be. Authors will tell you about the numerous drafts and redrafts they complete before they hand in the final manuscript.

To be efficient, you must have good time management. You are able to evaluate which tasks are important and which are urgent to complete. You are then able to allocate your time accordingly.

If you are unsure how you manage your time, keep a time diary for a few days. In your diary, write down how you spent your time for a period of twenty-four to forty-eight hours. After you complete your diary, look for regular patterns, areas where you use time effectively and where you waste it. From these results, make whatever changes are necessary.

3. Excellent

When you are carrying out a task, do you strive to be the best you can be? I know when I was teaching in school, some students would be satisfied with a C grade, as that was the level the government said they needed to leave school. Once they gained a C grade, they wouldn't strive to get anything higher. However, some students who gained an A grade were not happy because they wanted an A* grade.

When you look at excellence, you need to consider the time and the skills you have. You have to accept that one person's best will be different from another.

Which type of student will you be:

One who is satisfied with a C grade, or ☐

One who strives to gain an A* grade? ☐

4. Early

Do you leave things to the last minute, or do you give yourself enough time to be able to review your work? When I was writing this book, I booked six months with a coach to complete the manuscript. I produced a time plan as to how much writing I would complete each fortnight. I also had to ensure I had time to complete the first draft and then edit it. For most of the time, I was on schedule. You have to remember I was not just writing my book, I was also having to complete a lot of new tasks for my start-up business. I was constantly learning. I finished my manuscript on time, so we were able to review it at our last session. I made other changes to improve the quality of the book, including new learning which had taken place. If I had not prepared adequately, it would have taken me several years to complete this book, instead of months.

5. Enjoyable

How enjoyable are you to work with? Remember the students in the science investigation? Some of them were enjoyable to work with, and others were not. Some of them were lazy and wouldn't produce any work, whilst others were very organised. The lazier students did not have a set of results to use; a technician would photocopy a set for them to use.

When you are in a work setting, are you a good member of the team? Do you carry out the tasks assigned to you within the timeframe allocated? Are you missed when you are not in work, because of the value you add to others?

Using the goals that you assigned yourself at the end of chapter 2, how would you score yourself for each of these five areas? For example, a score of 0 means that you are not enthusiastic, whereas 10 means that you are very enthusiastic.

Good Attitude	Score out of 10
Enthusiastic	
Efficient	
Excellent	
Early	
Enjoyable	

How would you summarise your attitude?

Excellent ☐   Very Good ☐   Good ☐   Requires Improvement ☐

What Did Your Score Show about Your Level of Attitude?

In order for me to strive for excellence, I needed to engage in training to acquire new skills. I had to admit to myself I could not do everything, so I sourced the best help I could afford. As I gained the training, I found myself moving from my comfort zone to my stretch zone. This happened frequently, and I developed a more positive attitude about my own personal goals. I no longer wanted to return to my original comfort zone, as I realised it was limiting my growth. You too may have found, as you engage in new activities and see the positive benefits in your life, you don't want to return to your comfort zone. You are like a snake that has outgrown its old skin, and so it sheds it to allow the new one to grow.

I also had to review if the goals I set myself were S.M.A.R.T. goals. I had to be realistic with all of the things I was doing. I learnt it was better to concentrate on a few things and do them well and get help with the other tasks. I did not need to compete. I also learnt better time management skills. For example, I wouldn't set myself a goal to finish a task in two weeks when realistically I knew that it would take me at least a month. These more accurate timeframes meant I was not overstretched, and therefore my stress was more manageable.

What Does S.M.A.R.T. Stand For?

Specific: The goal needs to be specific rather than general.

Measurable: How can you measure the progress that you are making towards your goal?

Attainable: Have you attained the attitudes, abilities, and skills to help you reach your goals?

Realistic: Is the goal realistic: something that you are willing and able to achieve with the right training?

Timely: Do you have a timeframe to ensure you have a sense of urgency?

How I Applied These S.M.A.R.T. Targets to Writing This Book

I could have procrastinated and said, "I don't need to finish writing according to my time plan." I could have kept putting it off till tomorrow, instead of sitting at my computer and writing my thoughts or recording them with a voice recorder. However, I knew tomorrow never comes. As

I competed the work according to my schedule, I was in a position to get the assistance I needed to review the chapter I had written and then plan how I would write the next chapter. It also meant I was getting a better service from my book coach. At each coaching session, I allocated time to discuss the book and marketing strategies. I wanted to ensure I was getting good value for my money. If every time I had to do my part, I came up with excuses why I hadn't finished the next chapter, then the quality of the book would have suffered. Why? Because each session was discussed by two people and not just one. She allowed me to check the clarity of my work and also to go into more depth with a particular topic or to look for alternative ways to say the same thing. My coach also helped me soften my writing style so it was not so academic. This was my hardest challenge, but as you can see, I was able to change my style (most of the time).

What Happens if You Apply This Learning in the Real World?

What happens if you adopt the right attitude in your personal as well as in your professional life? I know when my sons arrive home from work, it's not a good time for me to have a conversation with them, especially if they had a long journey home or are feeling hungry. I know I need to give them space to de-stress, and then we can talk later. If I tried to have a conversation with them when they first arrive home, I could say they had a bad attitude, when in fact it was me who was not considering their needs.

In the previous chapter, we discussed the topic of engagement. Engagement and attitude go hand-in-hand. If you do not have the right attitude, then your outcomes will not be as favourable. We have come to another pivotal moment in the book. The question you must reflect on next is, Are you going to have a negative attitude or a positive one? Before you make a choice, let's look at some traits of a negative attitude.

Examples of Negative Attitudes

1. Overconfident

Are you able to accept the views of others, or do you always think that your way is the best way? Do you say, "I have always completed a task a particular way, and I get the results that I need, so why should I change now?"

2. Impatient

Are you willing to allow things to happen in a given time, or do you want to speed up the process? Have you ever seen a two-year-old having a tantrum? Most of the time, they want to do something they haven't acquired the skills for; they are not prepared to be assisted or shown what to do. Are you still behaving like a two-year-old, when you cannot have your own way?

3. Stubborn

Do you always want things your way? Are you not prepared to allow someone else to share their ideas? Are you not willing to learn something new? Imagine what your life would be like if you did not learn how to use a computer or mobile phone. As we go into more and more businesses, we can see roles that used to be carried out by people are now being automated. Some banks and fast food restaurants have even replaced tills with automated computer systems. If you are stubborn to change, then you will be left behind. Technology is going to keep advancing; it's becoming an integral part of our life, whether you like it or not.

4. Procrastination

Do you automatically put off tasks to another time? If you do this occasionally, it's not a problem, but if it's a habit, then this is a negative attitude. If you keep procrastinating, in the end it will increase your stress level, as you will have to produce work in a shorter period of time. Also, the quality of your work wouldn't be the best, as you wouldn't have enough time to work effectively.

5. Disbelief

Do you listen to negative advice of others? When others say that you cannot do a task, do you believe them? When I decided to change careers, it would have been easy to stay within my comfort zone. I knew that my work was not challenging me, and I was not making a difference in the lives of others. I wasn't being stretched, and my work was making me feel really depressed and low. I had learnt from my experiences; my attitude was critical to my outcome. Even though it would have been easy to abandon my dream and return to the classroom full-time, I did not; I knew that the bigger picture was worth the struggles for the short time.

Summary

In this chapter, we have learnt the following:

- The characteristics of people who have good attitudes,
- The benefits of having the right attitude in the workplace and at home,
- Examples of negative attitudes, and
- The link between engagement and attitude and how they influence the final outcome in a specific situation.

Action Points

- Using the notes you made from your time of reflection, write down some specific things that you can do to improve your attitude.
- Review your goal that you set the end of chapter 2 and revise it, if necessary, to ensure that it's a S.M.A.R.T. goal.

Chapter 6

ARE YOU IN THE MAJORITY
OR IN THE MINORITY?

Introduction

I was back in training again as a Master Coach and attending a quarterly workshop. I arrived early at the hotel venue and was greeted by the trainer, who made me feel very relaxed. I was introduced to the others who were attending, and we socialised. As we waited, I wondered where our other colleagues were. Just after eleven o'clock, we were shown into the room the training was taking place in. It was then I realised we were having an intimate training session. I counted the chairs: sixteen.

Although about a hundred people had attended the previous training, only a few of us had taken the step to move onto the next level. We had become a masterclass: the minority.

When we hear the words "minority" and "majority," we always make the assumption that being in the majority is the better of the two. However, I am discovering more and more, as I venture out of my comfort zone into my stretch zone, being in the minority can be the best place to be.

As a member of this masterclass for coaches, I was learning skills to take my business to the next level. I was also able to share ideas with other people who also wanted to grow, both personally and professionally.

As the training progressed, we looked at the impact in our lives of making daily affirmations. It was one of the techniques we had been taught at the last training. We were asked the question, "How many of you are using daily affirmation?"

I put up my hand.

Then we were told, "Those of you who put up your hand, please stand."

Three of us stood up.

Three out of fifteen. I realised that I was a minority of the minority. I was one of the 20 percent instead of the 80 percent.

What Is An Affirmation?

An affirmation is when you speak your subconscious thoughts out loud. They are used to build positive thoughts, by using positive speech, which results in positive actions. For my daily affirmation, I start by addressing the higher power I believe controls my life. Other people address a universal force. I then discuss what burdens I want to remove from my life. These were the burdens for me:

1. The fear of returning to the comfort zone I had left behind when I decided to have a career change.
2. The fear of not having the skills to be successful.
3. The fear of not fitting in the new circles of influence I was now an integral part of.

The latter part of the affirmation allowed me to say what I wanted to replace these fears with. This has been the most powerful part of using affirmations for me. I have seen doors open for me I would never have dreamt of, like being a television presenter. I am also attracting people towards me like a magnet attracts metal. These people are helping me to take my business to another level.

These revelations help me to realise it's good to be different from others. There are benefits of being in the minority and not the majority. I also realised one was not better than the other, but the choices I made required me to choose if I was going to be in the majority or the minority. I could not sit on the fence.

In the previous chapters, you looked at the benefits of being an active listener instead of a passive listener. This is the **L** part of L.E.A.R.N. You looked at the benefits of being engaged: the **E** part of L.E.A.R.N. In the last chapter, you looked at your attitude, the **A** of L.E.A.R.N. In this chapter, you are going to explore the benefits of reflecting and making your own choices about actions you will take. You need to decide if you will follow the crowd or be different. Do you want to be in the majority or in the minority: the **R** part of L.E.A.R.N.?

Reflections of Learning

Before we go any further, let's reflect on what we have learnt so far. This book has presented exercises for you to complete to apply the learning to your own personal or professional goals. Have you completed the exercises and action points at the end of each chapter, or are you putting them off to complete at a later date?

If you haven't completed the exercises, then you are in the majority of readers who are reading this book. If you have completed them, then you are in the minority.

If I know most readers will not complete the exercises in the book, why do I include them? Wouldn't it be better to leave them out?

If I was focusing on the majority of readers, then it would be true: I wouldn't include application exercises in this book, but because I want the minority to grow and be transformed as they read this book, I included the different exercises and activities, so the minority of my readers could develop more. I did this because I know the benefit the activities would have on their personal development. I know because this is how I learn. These deep learners will want to apply what they are learning personally, using the technique of active learning as discussed in chapter 2. Remember: Active learning is learning in bite-size chunks, but also applying the learning straight away to a given task of your choosing. As you use active learning, it will result in your own personal development.

You have seen this before; an event occurs, and witnesses are asked to give their account of what happened. Although the accounts would be similar, each one would focus on a different part of the event, subconsciously; as a result, all of their accounts would be different. The same is true for our learning. Although we are all reading the same text, I know some of you will gain one key thought, whilst another person will gain another idea. It doesn't matter what idea we learn; what matters is we learn something we can apply to our own lives and individual situations.

Ambition

If you are an active learner and always want to learn new things, then others around you may describe you as being ambitious. Would your family and friends describe you as an ambitious person? Even though you are in a good job, are you always striving to move up the career ladder?

If your current company cannot meet your needs, are you looking for a new role in a new company? Are you striving for excellence? When others observe you, do they wonder what's driving you?

If you were to interview driven people, you will observe they have four characteristics in common. They have **passion** for what they are doing. You can hear and see this in most of their conversations. At every opportunity, they share what new things are happening with them to reach their goals. They have a **positive mindset**. They are always looking for ways to better themselves, and they concentrate on the small details. With all of the learning they are doing, they put the training into practice. They do not just have ideas in their head; they are **doers**. The final characteristic is they are **very competitive**. They want to be the top in everything they do. They want to be number one.

Developing Self-Esteem

You may not describe yourself as an ambitious person. You may be reading this book to develop your self-esteem. You may be feeling a little bit uncomfortable about being described as ambitious; that is fine too. However, I would like you to reflect for a few minutes on where these emotions are coming from.

Let me share a bit more about my own personal journey. After I made the decision that I wasn't going back to school in September, I then had to go and learn new skills. I attended training courses in person and also as webinars. I found as I attended these courses, I was meeting people from different backgrounds; they were very different from my colleagues in the education field. Despite that fact that we came from different backgrounds, we had similar goals and wanted to grow our businesses.

The more networking meetings I attended, the more confident I became. The nerves would still be there, especially if I was attending a meeting where I did not know anyone, but I knew it was something I had to do. As I networked, doors started to open for me. Initially, I would discuss what I was doing but not the real reason. After one of these events, I was asked the why question: "Why did you leave teaching after twenty-five years to set up your own company? Wouldn't it have been easier to stay in teaching with all of the experience you have?" Eventually, I started to share the emotional breakdown I had at work and the emotional trauma I went through afterwards. I said that I wanted to be there to support others who were going though similar challenges.

This was my lightbulb moment. At my first business exhibition event, I learnt about the Well-being Charter for businesses. A few days later, a writer called me and used my business in an article about the importance of well-being in the workplace. Were all of these events coincidental, or were they an answer to my daily affirmation and my willingness to deal with my fears? Despite all of this positive energy surrounding me, I still had some personal internal challenges I needed to deal with. I started to explore where these feelings were coming from.

As I explored, I realised a lot of my thoughts were to do with my upbringing. Many women in my family went into either nursing or teaching. No one had been a business owner. Everyone had always worked in the public sector, in one occupation or another. I was stepping out from the norm and from what I was expected to do. From a child, I had been conditioned that you go to school and get a good education. You then go to university, and once you graduate, you get a good job. In this job, you will be promoted, and when you reach retirement age, you will retire with a good pension.

This bubble has been burst for many. There are no more jobs for life. There are fewer public sector jobs. Pensions are not enough, so many people are working past the age of sixty-five. Consequently, more people are finding themselves in challenging situations not of their own choice. They are having to step out of their comfort zones and try new things. You too may be stepping out of your norm. Your parents wanted you to become a doctor, so you went and achieved your degree for them. You were not happy as you completed your studies because, in your heart, you wanted to go into a creative job. Even today, some students are not able to choose their own subjects, due to pressure from their peers, parents, or teachers.

Are you being held back from pursuing your goal because you don't want to be different from what others expect of you? What is that inner voice saying to you?

> *"Listen to your inner voice, and do not let anyone stop you from being the person you know, within, you need to be."*

From my personal experiences, because I persevered with my new career direction, others have observed that I am passionate about what I am doing. A new Ruth has emerged, just like a butterfly coming out of a cocoon, a Ruth who is happy within. I have a positive mindset. I have learnt I am stronger by sharing with others how I feel, and I ask for help in areas I don't have skills in. Don't get me wrong; I have learnt so many new skills, especially around the use of social media to get others to know about me and my business. I am learning what I need to do, so that my business is a success and not a failure. I have had to spend time refining what I want my core message to be, and I have been praised because I am prepared to learn from others.

As I shared my experiences with others, I realised why I missed working in the school I had been made redundant from. I was not just a teacher; I was also spending quality time with the students as a parent figure. I spoke about challenges the students were facing and how I was able to guide them as a mentor. I was changing lives and helping many students aim for higher goals than they thought possible. The thought of going to university and completing a degree seemed an impossible task for many. Now when I speak with their peers or see some of them at social events, I feel proud when I am told how well they are doing. I regularly say if I did not make the decision to leave my comfortable school and work in an inner London school, which had a lot of problems, then most of these students would have followed the norm and been in the majority and not the minority. Some of these students were the first member of their family to go into higher education. That was a great accomplishment for them, and they proudly showed me their graduation pictures.

As I spoke with these challenging students, one of the reasons they gave for their poor behaviour was they wanted to be noticed in class. They wanted to feel important. Others could not read or write confidently or carry out other tasks in the classroom; they misbehaved so it would be a distraction. They felt that their family did not care about them, so why should we as teachers? Despite a lack of family finances, they were given the latest clothes and technology as a sign of love, when in effect, they wanted quality time, without the mobile phones, with an adult who cared for them and put them first.

As I shared my teaching experiences with others, it resonated with them. I realised I had planted a seed in their minds, for them to think about how much quality time they had with family members, friends, or colleagues. Others were able to understand the concept, and they were learning why I had a passion for improving communication, especially using listening skills in the home, at work, or at play.

I began to think how different our families and businesses would be if we actually spent some quality time each day communicating with each other, having a conversation that involved active listening, instead of passive listening. What would happen if we were fully engaged in finding out the needs and goals of others; if we had a positive attitude; if we supported others to follow their dreams (even if their dreams were different from what we thought they should be)? Then we would have more people in the minority than the majority. The percentage of people in each group would be closer, as more people would be working towards their own personal goals.

What would have happened if I did not make the decision to step out of my comfort zone and learn new skills? What would have happened if I stayed in the classroom, doing a job I no longer enjoyed? What would have happened if I did not share with others how I was feeling over certain things and got the help that I needed?

You too may have a lot of questions you need to clarify. In the space below, write down some of the thoughts you are thinking right now. It's always good to write down your thoughts from your head, as you are more likely to act on them.

In chapter 1, you were asked four questions, and for each one, you needed to select response (a), (b), or (c).

Question One

You attend a training course about an area of work that you identified during your appraisal meeting. Do you

(a) not attend because the notice given to you was too short?
(b) attend and engage with the tasks set during the training?
(c) attend and apply the knowledge to the area that you identified in your appraisal when you return to work?

Question Two

You attend a training seminar and receive a manual with useful information. What do you do with the manual once you return to work?

(a) Put it on a shelf or in your filing cabinet.
(b) Go over the notes that you made to reinforce the learning you received.
(c) Go over your notes and then share the main points learnt with other colleagues.

Question Three

You are looking for a new job and find a role that you have always wanted to do. As you read the job description, you are unsure if you have all of the skills and standards required. Do you

(a) decide not to apply for the job because you tell yourself that you will not be shortlisted?
(b) apply and wait to see if you are shortlisted for the interview?
(c) contact the company to gain clarification, and then use the information given to complete the application and apply for the role?

Question Four

You are asked to attend the interview. On your arrival, you see that you are one of six candidates for the post. As you share information with each other, you feel the other five candidates are more experienced than you. What do you do next?

(a) After you complete the first selection task, which you found difficult, you withdraw from the selection process.

(b) You complete all of the selection tasks to the best of your ability.

(c) You complete the selection tasks to the best of your ability, and during the interview stage, you answer all of the questions confidently, using information that you researched about the company.

Which responses would a person who acted in the majority give? Which responses would someone in the minority give?

Using the responses above, people who want to be ambitious, make the most of opportunities they are given, and move from procrastination to action would

- attend the training course about an area of work they identified as part of their appraisal, even though the notice was short. Once they returned to work, they would apply what they have learnt so they were able to produce work of a better quality.

- regularly review the notes they made during the training which are found in their manual, and they would apply the learning to their work or when they trained other staff.

- apply for a new job after they have contacted the company to gain clarification. They would then use the information gained during the interview. Even if they were not successful, they would know they were fully prepared, and they would use the experiences gained when they apply for their next role.

- complete all of the tasks given during the interview, and they would ask for further information as they had informal conversations with key staff. They would want to have a lot of relevant information about the company, because they would be making a conscious decision if they wanted to work for the company. Most people forget an interview is a two-way process.

How Would This Compare With Others?

- They would not attend the training course, as they were not given enough notice.
- They would put the manual on a shelf and not open it again.
- They would decide not to apply for any jobs they felt they were not qualified for.
- They would withdraw from any interview in which they found the selection tasks too difficult.

Both groups of people make the choice as to what their outcome will be. They decide if they want to stay in the status quo or step out and do something different. They decide if they want to follow the norm or stand out from the crowd. Whatever choice they make, there will be consequences.

What decisions are you going to make? What changes, if any, are you going to implement? Let me assure you that when I made my decision to change, it was not an easy one. I first had to change my mindset on a number of things. As the months passed, I had to look at my situation and refine how I did things. At each stage, I knew why I was taking certain actions, so that helped me with the transition. I also had to keep my immediate family in the loop because they were affected by my actions, directly or indirectly. In the end, I found a coach to hold me accountable for decisions I made but also to boost my confidence when I was having a low day. This coach is the same one I met back at the start of this chapter. She also wrote the foreword of this book.

We are nearing the end of this book. The next chapter will be the last one. At this time, you may want to review the five steps we discussed in chapter 2, so you can move from procrastination to action.

Step 1. **Start**. Review and decide where you want to be and set about achieving it. Do you want to be in the majority or the minority?

It would be good for you to carry out an audit at this time to write down the reasons for and against each group.

Reasons **for** being in the **majority** group	Reasons **for** being in the **minority** group
Reasons **against** being in the **majority** group	Reasons **against** being in the **minority** group

Step 2. **Team**. Surround yourself with a supportive team to help you work towards your goal.

Step 3. **Emotions**. Be honest with yourself and others about the choices and actions you want to take in your life. Be aware: You may not be supported with your choices and actions. You may have to journey alone, for a while, until you can get others on board or become part of a new circle of influence.

Step 4. **Positivity**. If you have made the decision you want to be in the minority, then do something positive toward your goal. If you decide that you want to remain the majority and leave things as they are or to make the rate of transition slower, celebrate, as that too is a good decision. You decide what decision is the best for you at this current time.

Step 5. **Success**. Share with at least two people a goal you have set for yourself and ask them to hold you accountable for working towards achieving it. In the end, you are more likely to be successful. I know that if I did not have a coach who gave me clear, short deadlines to complete a certain portion of this book each fortnight, I would be like many authors: part way through their first draft and unsure if I could finish writing the book.

How Can You Stand out from the Crowd?

When I was younger, I often heard the saying "Birds of a feather flock together"; the adults in my circle of influence wanted to remind me it was important to have friends who would be a positive influence in my life. I also encouraged my sons to choose their friends carefully.

As you get older and choose your own friends and your own occupation, it's sometimes easier to just blend in with others, as you may not want to stand out in the crowd. That quality is fine if you want to be in the majority, but if you want to be in the minority, you may have to do things in a different way.

One way you stand out is in your relationships with others. When I had the role of deputy head teacher, my students always said that I never used my position to get them to complete a particular action. They said I taught them to do things because it was the right thing. I taught them to respect themselves and others. They said this made me stand out.

As I progressed in my career, I learnt about the importance of good relationships in management. If you have a good relationship with your staff and they feel valued, they will go the extra mile for you. Remember scenario one, the late phone call from chapter 4? If Dave's boss valued him, then he would stay and finish the report. If Dave did not have a good relationship with his boss, he would leave work at 5 p.m. Doesn't everyone want to be valued? Isn't this what we want from all of our relationships? We want to be able to lean on them and talk honestly with them.

These are good reasons to be in the minority. The minority make a positive difference in the lives of others. They make a valuable difference in our own lives and in the organisation. What a difference it would make in businesses if better relationships were the norm. This would result in better productivity in the workplace; fewer sick days would be taken off.

There are other consequences of standing out in the crowd. It may mean your friendship groups may change, because you now want a different way of life than you had in the past. You may be spending more time in personal development activities instead of leisure. Your friends may not fully understand the reasons why you are choosing to use your time differently. As hard as the decision may be, you may decide you need new friends in your life who will support you with your new choices.

The changes you make may only be personal to you. However, it's important to follow up on any specific decisions you have made. When I had my emotional meltdown, I initially did not share the real reason why I was home. It took me several months to let close friends know I was back in counselling. I knew for myself I had buried too many emotions which were impacting me subconsciously. However, due to the training I was receiving as part of my Master Coach support, they had come to the surface. I had a choice to make. I decided I had to honestly address these issues. I knew it would be painful at times, but I also knew from my counselling training that the benefits would outweigh the pain.

When you are facing challenges, it's so easy to not be honest with yourself, but if you are, I have found it can impact all areas of our lives. It means when new opportunities come your way, which you would have run from in the past, you are now able to embrace them with open arms. You too will find as you step out from the crowd in one area of your life, and be in the minority instead of the majority, you are now able to accomplish your goals much easier in other areas of your life. The more you are the real you, the easier it will be next time to be truly authentic. You are developing new habits, habits which will put you in the 20 percent and not in the 80 percent of individuals.

What Are the Characteristics of People Who Like To Be in the Minority?

One of the first things you will notice about them is that they are confident. Even when things are not going as planned, they will be resilient and look for a solution. They have a "can do" attitude. They have an inner strength and a positive mindset. They also are realistic. They do not live with their heads in the sky. They pay attention to detail and have good time management. You will find these characteristics in the majority group too, but I have found that the level of commitment to their use is higher in the minority group.

Which Group Do You Want To Be In?

I have found I am naturally in the minority group, and for a long time, I thought most people were like me. However, I am often asked, How do I do what I do? How do I cope so well with the challenges in my life?

Inside, I don't feel like a role model, but I am realising that for many, I am. As I am getting to know the real me better, and as my circle of influence extends, I am becoming more confident to try new things and embrace new opportunities that are coming my way.

I know if you too start to make conscience changes in your life, you will start to change within. At first, the changes will be so small that you may not notice them.

Imagine you are a white egg on a cabbage leaf. You are one of many. You have just hatched. Out comes a green hairy caterpillar. You spend your days feeding and increasing in size. One day, you spin a cocoon around yourself and go into hibernation. You are not sure how long you are unseen by others, but one day, things change. The cocoon is too small, and so with a struggle, you break free. You soon realise you are flying. You are no longer in one place but you can soar high in the sky. When did these changes take place? How did these changes take place, because within you, you do not feel any different?

A similar transformation takes place when you are in the minority. One day, you realise you have fully changed and are now doing things you never imagined were possible. You are now ready for the final part of L.E.A.R.N. In the last chapter of the book, we will discuss the importance of planning what your next steps will be.

Summary

In this chapter, we have learnt the following:

- There are advantages of being in the minority.
- There are steps you can take to move from the majority into the minority.
- Being in the minority can impact your life.
- You can stand out in a crowd.
- A transformation takes place as you change from being in the majority to the minority.

Actions Points

- Make a decision to decide if you want to be in the majority or the minority.
- Make a list of areas of your life you want to improve and draw up a plan of action to show how and when you want to put these changes in place.
- Keep a diary or reflection journal to record the impact, both positive and negative, of the changes you are making in your life.

Chapter 7

NEXT STEPS

Introduction

What a journey we have been on. I cannot believe this is the last chapter of the book. I first thought about the outline of this book when I was home from work, recovering from the emotional meltdown I shared in chapter 2. I wanted something to do to take my mind off my situation. I did not contact work because of the pain I felt. I also wanted to understand why I was feeling so low emotionally, doing something I had enjoyed for as long as I can remember. Due to the pain that I was feeling, I was not being honest with myself or with those around me. I was feeling anger, an emotion I don't normally express.

This is why now, as I write this last chapter, I cannot believe how much I have grown and developed. I have embraced new opportunities which have come my way and have a quest to learn new things. The more I am learning, the more I want to learn. Don't get me wrong: I haven't been positive all through this journey, as you will have seen if you read all the chapters in this book.

Let me use an illustration to describe this journey. Have you ever been on a long, winding road in the countryside? You drive slowly down the road with your full beams on, because you are not sure where the next bend in the road is or how sharp it will be. Behind you are some local drivers who are just looking for an opportunity to overtake you and drive fast down the road. Once they get the opportunity, they put their foot down and they are gone, leaving you behind.

At this point in your journey, do you stop your car and say, "There is no point continuing my journey," or do you continue traveling at your own pace until you reach your destination?

You can apply this same principle to this book. It doesn't matter how long it takes you to complete your journey; what matters is that you arrive at your chosen destination.

Let me share with you another story. I left home to go to a retreat for businesswomen. I put the address in the satnav on my phone, connected my phone to my car charger (as I know using this particular app drains my battery quickly), and started on my journey. I went down all of the roads as the voice told me, and eventually it said, "You have reached your destination."

As I got out of the car, a lady came out and asked me what I wanted. I was at the wrong address. The farm I needed was down the road. I got back into the car and went to look for the farm. I found one, but it did not look like what I wanted, so I went back to the main road. I drove up and down the road, and before long, I realised I was lost. The Internet and my phone didn't work, as there was no signal. What was I going to do? I realised I needed help. I drove up the road until I saw a house and parked in the drive. The owner of the home came to the front door. I got out of my car and told him where I needed to go. He gave me clear instructions, and within ten minutes, I found my destination. The trainers were just about to come look for me, as they had got the message I had sent to them, saying I was lost.

You can be at any of the stages described above. You may know where you want to go and are traveling fast towards your goal. You may be traveling towards your goal and know the direction, but you are taking your time and learning from each part of the journey. You may have arrived at what you thought was the end and now find you have farther to go. Alternatively, you may be lost and now need the help of another person to get you back on track. It doesn't matter which route you take. What matters is that you reach your destination.

Recap

In chapter 1, we discussed the topic of motivation. There are a lot of things which work together to motivate you to complete a specific task. According to Maslow's hierarchy, your basic needs of food, water, and shelter have to be met first, before you can go on a journey of personal development.

Chapter 2 looked at the five steps that are needed to take action. After I wrote this chapter, I shared it with the attendees at one of my networking events. As I shared my business insight, they were given the opportunity to reflect on their achievements in the past year and to plan goals for what they want to achieve in the year ahead. When they looked at the aspect of TEAM, they realised the importance of having others around to support them, even if they were the only one employed.

Your goal may be to set up your own business. If you are used to working with others, the adjustment of working alone can make you feel lonely and even depressed. When you are completing your business plan, include how you are going to meet your social needs. As we have previously discussed, your mindset can affect outcomes and productivity. As we further discussed the five steps, we realised the steps are in fact five shifts in our thinking.

Step One. START. Unless you take the first step in any direction, you will be standing still. It's so easy to keep putting off making decisions, to procrastinate, but unless you do something, anything, then you cannot reach your goal.

Step Two. TEAM. Teamwork is important, because the members of your team not only support you, they hold you accountable for your decisions. If you have someone monitoring your progress towards your goal, then you are more likely to make the first step. You can now see how steps 1 and 2 complement each other. You may even have to do step 2 first: find yourself an accountability partner before you start your journey towards your goal.

Step Three. EMOTIONS. These can make or break a particular dream or goal. I am now more open to share honestly how I feel about certain situations. Before, when I was asked how I was feeling, I would reply, "I am okay," or "I am fine." Now I will be more specific: "I am having a good day today because …" "I am feeling a little annoyed today because …"

Do you now give your emotions a name? Are you being more real with your team to share how you feel about certain things that are happening in your life? Remember: Your team is anyone you have interactions with, professionally, personally, or socially, but as you work, **T**ogether, **E**veryone **A**chieves **M**ore.

Step Four. POSITIVITY. This has been one of the greatest shifts for me as I have written this book. I started this book when I was experiencing one of the lowest points in my life. I described it this way: "I was walking across a tightrope. However, there was no safety net. Due to all of the pressure and lack of focus and concentration, I fell off and ended up in the bottom of a deep hole. I could not get out, as I did not know how. I felt totally helpless and abandoned."

As I now write this final chapter, I am now embracing the numerous opportunities which are coming my way. Some of these opportunities have left me speechless and pinching myself to see if I am dreaming. As I have become more positive in my mindset, people who have positive energy are attracted to me. The saying "Birds of a feather flock together" is so true. What positive shifts are happening to you right now? It's always good to name them and record them in a book or on your phone or wherever you keep important information.

Step Five. SUCCESS. What new successes are happening in your life right now? It's good to think about past success, but for personal growth, you need to have current successes as well. These will motivate you to keep striving towards your goal and your own personal finish line. These successes do not have to be major things. You just need to acknowledge to yourself and to others the new changes which are taking place in your life.

Before we continue with this chapter, this would be a good time for you to spend some time reflecting on your own personal journey. In the busyness of your personal and professional lives, it's difficult to find some personal space to reflect on yourself. You are always thinking about the needs of others or how you are going to complete tasks needed for your survival; you have little time to just stop and think and take stock personally.

I have found that even if I spend as little as five minutes a day having some "me" time, it makes a big difference to how I feel. Instead of reading the paper, I use the time for personal development. This may involve catching up with reading a book, listening to an audio, or writing down my thoughts about certain things that are happening in my life. I also use the time that I would spend watching television. Another technique is going to bed earlier at night, as I find I am now waking up earlier but refreshed. I then use the quietness of the night to reflect on the day which has passed and make plans for the next day. I was not an early morning person in the past. I knew others who would set their alarm for 4 or 5 a.m. and use this time for their personal development and reflection. I have adopted this new habit and feel good about rising early. Initially, you do not have to reflect each day; once or twice a week would be a good improvement. As you develop the habit and see how beneficial it is to you, then you will naturally want to have your me time more often.

How Can You Become More Motivated?

If you could spend a whole day doing whatever you liked to make you happy, what would be on your list?

How many things on your list do you already do, if any? What could you do to include some of these activities in your weekly or daily schedule?

In the media, we read stories of corporate executives who resign from their work to do a job that makes them happy. Others looking on would say they had given up a high salary, regular bonuses, a lot of perks: all of the things they strived to have. What they do not see was the late nights spent at work, the family gatherings they missed, the constant feeling of stress in their body, the lack of genuine support, and their lack of time at home.

So one day, they make a decision: They are going to take back control of their life. They are going to do something that makes them motivated to get out of bed in the morning. Do not get me wrong; I am not saying the executive lifestyle is always like this. Some people thrive in that environment, but for others, it becomes a burden. They feel as if they are chained to their work.

What Will Make You Happy?

In September 2015, I decided to have a career break. I had been working since the age of sixteen in a variety of jobs and occupations. I knew I was no longer happy working as a teacher but wondered how I could transfer my skills and knowledge to a new area. Some looking on thought I wouldn't be able to cope, because just like the executives, I was chained to my work. I lived and breathed teaching. However, it was no longer making me feel positive to get out of bed in the morning. I knew I still wanted to pass on knowledge and make a difference in the lives of others, but how?

The previous year, I had carried out a career survey when I was being assessed for what roles my skills were useful for. They came up with the roles of a being a trainer and a coach. I decided to train to be a certified Master Coach. As part of the training, I had to carry out a lot of self-reflection. As I delved deeper into the cause of some of the emotions I was feeling at the time, I noticed that my mindset started to change. I was feeling more positive.

It was with this positive energy that I went to the Business Show in December 2015, where I took part in a speed networking event. I had to pitch my business to another person for a minute, and then the person opposite me had to the same. This happened with fifteen other people. By the time I finished, I was feeling very exhausted but happy inside. I had learnt that I had so many dormant skills within me. If I had not taken the step to move out of my comfort zone and do something different, then I wouldn't have known what new things I was capable of doing. I would have thought all I could do was teach and work in a school environment. Don't get me wrong; there is nothing wrong with teaching as a career. I just knew I wanted to do something different with my life. I also knew that if I had not been made redundant and had the experiences which followed, I would probably still be teaching today.

One networking conversation was to open doors I would never have dreamt of. Someone I met told me one of his colleagues would be interested in speaking with me. After a few more conversations, I met with his colleague, who told me about a new community television programme he was working on for schools, families, and the local community. They were looking for someone to be a presenter. I did a test film but thought we were filming a promotion for my business. In hindsight, ignorance was bliss, because I was very relaxed as we filmed. After we finished filming my first scene, I learnt they wanted me to be one of the presenters of their new show. This would allow me to use my knowledge of education in a new way. I would be working directly with a professional television presenter on a variety of stories. I thought that I was dreaming. This was one of my ideal jobs. It used all of my skills: the old ones from my teaching career and the new ones as a trainer and coach. It would also give me a voice and allow me to make a difference in the lives of young people and families. This was the reason I had gone into teaching twenty-five years ago.

Imagine the joy I felt contacting the head teacher who had helped me with my development as a senior teacher, to ask him if I could come into his school to film. He agreed we could come and film one of his students as a reward. I arrived as part of the media team, and for the first time, I signed into the school's visitors book as something other than a teacher.

My co-presenter explained the project to the head teacher. As he spoke, I began to realise the project had expanded to become even bigger than I previously thought.

Before starting, the head teacher spoke with me as we walked to the room we were filming in. He asked me, "Ruth, how did you get involved in this project?"

I replied, "I was in the right place, at the right time, with the right skills which they needed."

I realised I now had the right mindset to embrace an opportunity which in the past I would have run from. The work with my Master Coach was transforming me. I now had a renewed sense of purpose each day. I am highly motivated, but this did not happen overnight. I had to put all of what I have written in this book into practice. I had to take my own medicine. I am glad I did, because new opportunities are opening for me each month.

You have a decision to make. No, I am not going to tell you to give up your job; I am just going to ask you a couple of personal questions: What would happen if you moved slightly out of your comfort zone and tried something new? What would happen if you applied the five steps to a new goal?

From your time of reflection, what would that new goal be? If you still have the original goal you set at the end of chapter 2, does it now have more depth? Or do you want to remain in your current situation, because you are motivated with what you are doing? One thing I have learnt: If something is not broken, it doesn't need to be mended. So if you are happy with your life as it is, do not make changes for change sake. However, if you know you want to grow in at least one area, then start to make the necessary changes.

How Can We Celebrate the Success that We Have Made?

Let's explore if you need to make any changes. Let me ask you another question: What do you find yourself talking about most of the time?

Are you proud of your achievement? These could be things you have achieved in your personal or professional life or both. At the end of my seminars, I ask attendees to share with another person (or the group, if they are feeling brave) an achievement they are proud of. As they share, they stand or sit up tall. They answer confidently and have smiles on their faces.

I hope this is how you are feeling when you think about your achievements. As I see the changes in their behaviour, it also makes me feel proud, because I have created a safe environment for them to grow.

This is how the children felt the day we filmed in their school. They came into the library, wondering why they were asked to meet as a group, and left feeling proud because someone had recognised the differences they made in their individual families. I shared with them how much I respected and admired them. I knew how difficult their lives can be, as my sons had taken care of me from a young age after I was diagnosed with lupus and had regular flare-ups.

So how would you feel if you knew your choices were affecting the lives of others in a positive way? Wouldn't it make you stand tall? Wouldn't you feel that life is worthwhile? Wouldn't you feel motivated to repeat the task again, so that you can change more lives for the better? I now feel the work I am doing will make a bigger difference in the lives of many, not just students, but families, businesses, and even society.

We have so many great examples of people who have made a difference in the lives of others because they truly believed what they were doing was for the common good. We have Martin Luther King and his famous speech, "I Have a Dream." Another example is how Nelson Mandela and the people of South Africa struggled against apartheid. Even though he faced so many challenges, he totally believed in the cause for equality and eventually became the first black president of South Africa.

So what difference do you want to make in the world? It doesn't have to be on the same scale as Martin Luther King or Nelson Mandela. If you stopped what you were doing, would there be a gap? Would you be missed? If you answered yes, then you know you are affecting change in your part of the world.

Isn't that one of the reasons why we do what we do? Don't we want to impact the lives of others in a positive way? Don't we want to make the world a better place?

I realised when I had my big emotional meltdown that it was partly caused because I knew I was not making a difference in the lives of my students. I had not changed, but the students had a different agenda; they were not into learning, and they were proud to tell me the games they played with staff. This also explained why the closing of the school was so profound; I had been part of the senior management team, and the emotional experiences of packing the students' files but not knowing where they would be attending next was also profound. Even now, thinking about my closed school and the lives we were changing makes me sad. I knew at least in my other school, I was safe, and the teachers were respected. I also knew if my school had not closed, I would still be teaching, and this book wouldn't have been written.

I also wouldn't have known that I had all of these talents hidden within me. So strange as it may sound, I have to thank the students who forced me to take back control of my life. What they did was wrong and should never have happened, but some good came out of it. I refused to be a victim. I chose to be a victor. I chose to say yes to new opportunities.

I realise I've come full circle. I've got a moral purpose again. I'm doing something I like, and the work I'm doing is creating change, not just in me but in the lives of others. In order for me to be where I am now, I had to step out from the crowd. I had to be in the minority and not the majority. I had to become an active learner and not a passive learner. I needed to engage with others because I realised I did not have some of the skills needed to succeed in my new roles. As I started to achieve success in one area of my life, I realised this new success was impacting other areas of my life.

Have you seen dominoes placed on a table so they are standing up with a small gap in between each one? They all look disconnected. That is, until the first one falls. It then touches the next domino, and before long, you have a chain reaction. One by one, the dominoes fall in order. This is what we have achieved in this book. We have connected a series of events in our lives and used them to improve our current and future situations.

Another analogy that you can use is a jigsaw puzzle. Each piece on its own is not significant. But when you join them all together, the right way, you have a beautiful picture to admire.

This book covered the following topics:

1. What is motivation?
2. S.T.E.P.S.: The Five-Step Strategy.
3. How do we listen effectively?
4. How do we become more engaged?
5. How do we have the right attitude?
6. How do we become the minority and not the majority?
7. How do we make the commitment to take the next steps?

We were able to see how we can have different outcomes when opportunities come our way.

What are you waiting for? Say yes to new opportunities!

Summary

In this chapter, we have learnt the following:

- You are on a journey of personal development; the route doesn't matter, nor does the time you take. What matters is you arrive at the chosen destination.
- There are ways you can become more motivated.
- There are things you can do to make you feel happier.
- It's important to have regular "me" time.
- You can celebrate the success you have made and plan for future successes.

Action Points

My logo contains the image of a butterfly; it represents the transformation which can occur in your life. For your final task, I would like you to summarise your learning by answering a series of questions. These questions parallel the different stages of a butterfly:

Egg stage. How would you describe yourself before you started to read this book?

Caterpillar stage. What new ideas have you learnt?

Chrysalis stage. How have you applied your new learning to your life?

Butterfly stage. What new things are you going to achieve now that you have wings and are able to fly and experience new opportunities?

Conclusion

Together, we have been on a journey of personal growth. As I wrote this book, a lot of transformations have taken place in my own life, both personally and professionally, in a relatively short period of time. When I first had the idea for this book, I was recovering at home after my emotional meltdown. I had asked myself the questions, "*Why do some students want to learn in school and others do not? Why do some want to use the opportunity of having free education whilst others do not appreciate what they have?*"

A few years ago, I went on a trip to The Gambia with three other teachers. We went to support our partner school. When we arrived, we realised the students had just the basic equipment. We were using a blackboard and chalk, not the interactive whiteboards we have in most of our schools in the UK. Each lesson a register was taken, not for the student but by one of the students, to show that a teacher had turned up and taught them that lesson. As I taught them maths and science, I commented to the other teachers, "These students do not have the same facilities we have in the UK, but they want to achieve. They are not pleased unless they are getting A grades. There is so much cooperation between the students as they teach each other. They want them all to do well." The last day, we took a picture with all of the teachers in the school. The classes were left unattended. The students had a high level of self-discipline.

They also had a "can do" attitude. They wanted to be the best they could be. They not only thought about "me," they also thought about "we." This was so different from the classes I was teaching when I had my meltdown. At one time, the British education system was the envy of many, but over the years, we have lost that reputation. Changes in the education system are the topic for another book.

I also realised that even though the school I was made redundant from was small and did not have as many resources as some of the bigger school, we were making a positive difference in the lives of the students. We were instilling in them the importance of having values, working together as a team, and striving for excellence: the same themes that we have covered in this book.

As you have read this book, you used the technique of accelerated learning. You have transferred the learning of each chapter to your own personal situation. You have become a more active learner and have shown you are a lifelong learner.

Like some of the attendees at my seminars, you may have found this style of learning difficult at first. It's not easy to take time to reflect deeply, focus on where you are now in your life, and determine the steps you need to take to get to the next level. If you have found the process difficult, don't be hard on yourself, just go back, reread the book, and complete the exercises when you are ready. Adult learning is different than learning in a classroom; you have more choices regarding how and when you will learn.

The first choice you made was to decide you wanted to make the most of opportunities that came your way. Once you made the start, you then surrounded yourself with people who wanted to help you along this journey. You chose your team. Dealing with your emotions was one of the hardest things you had to do. It would have been easier to dwell on the effects of events which had happened in your life, but for real personal growth, you needed to look at the causes.

The Circle of Blame exercise in chapter 4 really helped me to distinguish between the causes and effects of challenges in our lives. It can also help you to subjectively evaluate events which have happened in your life. It's useful to think about your past successes and use them to support your new goals. A positive mindset is important here. I discussed this more in chapter 6.

Finally, I reached the end of the journey. As I looked back, I was able to say confidently I had now succeeded in another area of my life. I had applied the five-step strategy to motivate myself to take action. It was no longer just a theoretical strategy I learnt about in chapter 2, but a tool that I could use and apply to a variety of different situations in my life.

You now know the importance of taking action. You are able to have a different response than the majority of people, when opportunities come your way. You have also learnt the skills to be active listeners. As this has now become a habit, you now have better relationships, as you are using more effective communication skills. You are more committed in your activities, both personally and professionally. You have examined what your core values are and established their importance. You have also examined in detail what can happen in your life if you have the right attitude. You have explored the advantages of not staying in the crowd and why being in the minority can be a good place to be. Finally, you have discovered new ways to reach your own goals.

If you put these strategies in place, you will be better motivated. Like my students in The Gambia, you will have high aspirations in your personal and professional lives. You will not only have higher aspirations; you will also have the skills to say yes when remarkable opportunities are presented to you.

If you have completed the action point tasks at the end of each chapter, you will have a record of the transformational changes which have taken place as you have read this book and applied the learning to your own unique situation. Like me, I am sure you too have accomplished things you thought were impossible.

As you have been on this transformational journey, a lot of learning has occurred as you have started to say yes to new opportunities and started to L.E.A.R.N.

Now that you have finished reading this interactive book, you may wonder what the next step is. How can you put the learning from this book into practice in your own life? Can you share additional information with me and others? In answer to these questions, I have developed a coaching programme called "Celebrate Your Uniqueness." This programme is a series of seven mini-courses; they can be taken as separate modules, but to have the greatest impact, they are best studied as a complete course over a period of months. Information about this course is available on my website. Are you unhappy at work and with the quality of your life? You do not have to settle for second-best. You can start to make changes that will allow you to get off the treadmill and start to take back control of your life.

Celebrate Your Uniqueness

These are the modules which will be covered in the full course:

1. Say yes to a better work-life balance.
2. Say yes to letting go of the past.
3. Say yes to letting go of fears.
4. Say yes to new opportunities.
5. Say yes to L.E.A.R.N.
6. Say yes to a healthier you.
7. Say yes to choosing a new you.

I hope you do not stop your personal development journey and you continue to soar and achieve great things in your life. For the final time, say yes to new opportunities.

Useful Links

In the book, I have referred to a number of organisations which helped me say yes to new opportunities. As promise, I have placed the links below.

1. Listening to Your Voice website. https://www.listeningtoyourvoice.co.uk/
2. Ruth Pearson personal website. http://www.ruthpearsonuk.com/
3. Celebrate Your Uniqueness. http://eepurl.com/cvkZ1n
4. Master Coach Training https://mastercoach.co/home-page?gclid=CLiFsMyw5s4CFdcK0wodwcQFMA
5. Motivational Maps. http://www.motivationalmaps.com/
6. Good News Britain. http://www.goodnewsbritain.com/
7. The National Wellbeing Charter. http://www.wellbeingcharter.org.uk/index.php
8. The London Healthy Wellbeing Charter. https://www.london.gov.uk/what-we-do/health/healthy-workplace-charter
9. Your Business Community. https://www.yourbusinesscommunity.co.uk/
10. 4 Networking.biz. https://www.4networking.biz/forum
11. The Mumpreneurs Networking Club http://www.mumpreneursnetworkingclub.co.uk/
12. London Professionals. https://www.londonprofessionals.co.uk/
13. The Speakers Associates. https://www.speakersassociates.com/speaker/ruth-pearson
14. Coach Me Smart. http://coachmesmart.com/

Connect with me via social media

Linked In: https://uk.linkedin.com/in/ruthpearsonltyv

Facebook: https://www.facebook.com/Listening-To-Your-Voice-Limited-745322678920748/

Twitter: https://twitter.com/LTYV_Ltd

Email: ruth.pearson@listeningtoyourvoice.co.uk

About the Author

Ruth Pearson is an inspirational coach, motivational speaker, television presenter, and author who motivates others so they too can be inspired to aspire. Her career started in an educational setting, and she later learnt about the use of the Motivational Maps system and trained to be a Master Coach. Her coaching helps others to get detailed understanding of what motivates them as individuals, their colleagues, or the teams that they are part of.

Ruth is passionate about supporting people so they can be motivated to learn, in both their personal and professional lives. She wants individuals to learn strategies and then apply them to new opportunities when they arrive. She also wants them to learn to stand out from the crowd and be one of the minority and not the majority.

Ruth has a vision: to establish a network of collaborative services that will assist individuals and businesses with techniques to motivate others and equip them with life skills. She also believes that individuals should look after their own well-being. She wants to take the strategies taught in this book into educational establishments so young people can learn the true value of education. Education is about teaching life skills through a variety of subjects. These skills are then applied in personal and professional roles. These life skills are academic knowledge, emotional intelligence, and communication skills, which in combination lead to highly motivated, productive, and engaged individuals.

Ruth is available to speak in the UK, where she resides, and internationally. She speaks on issues of empowering individuals to be the best that they can be, despite challenging situations that they may find themselves in. She shares her own personal life experiences in a way that helps others to know that they do not have to let their past define their future. She shares specific strategies they can use to be motivated to take action, have better relationships (both personally and professionally), and have a better work-life balance.

She can be contacted via her website: www.listeningtoyourvoice.co.uk or via social media.